E. Cowley

The Writers of Genesis and Related Topics

Illustrating Divine Revelation

E. Cowley

The Writers of Genesis and Related Topics
Illustrating Divine Revelation

ISBN/EAN: 9783337778576

Printed in Europe, USA, Canada, Australia, Japan

Cover: Foto ©Lupo / pixelio.de

More available books at **www.hansebooks.com**

THE
WRITERS OF GENESIS

AND RELATED TOPICS, ILLUSTRATING DIVINE REVELATION.

BY

REV. E. COWLEY, D.D.,

AUTHOR OF "BIBLE GROWTH AND RELIGION," "GOD IN CREATION," AND "GOD ENTHRONED IN REDEMPTION."

"God spake unto Noah, and to his sons, and to Abraham, this covenant."

NEW YORK:
THOMAS WHITTAKER,
2 AND 3 BIBLE HOUSE.
1890.

PREFACE.

When abroad, in 1872, I read in the *Daily Telegraph* Mr. George Smith's Chaldean Account of the Creation, which he had just deciphered. Previous knowledge of Layard's discoveries enabled me to estimate their importance, and to continue the study of Oriental discoveries. So, in 1879, I ventured to give a brief series of sermons on the Religion and Learning of Egypt in the era of Moses, in the Church of the Heavenly Rest, New York.

A few years later, Mr. Spencer, in his "Ecclesiastical Institutions," struck off the roots of the Divine in Religion. As no one else appeared to answer him, I felt bound (God being my helper) to examine and refute him, or yield to the inevitable.

In some other papers I have ventured to defend the Revelation of the Old Testament against the gross naturalism of Renan and the negative criticism of Kuenen and Wellhausen. Thus I have traversed some crucial points from Genesis to the Prophecies of our Lord.

This may best explain why I presume to add to what has been so ably—in some instances so foolishly—written upon the Origin of Genesis. I can but think that the reader will here find that the last word had not been said, and that the application of modern discoveries to the Oracles of God will flash the new light of His providence across them, and enable us to determine *who* were the writers of Genesis and of some other books.

The Right Rev. Bishop Perry, of Iowa, a most competent witness, reports that some members of the last Pan-Anglican Council had doubts of portions of the Bible, notably Genesis, which illustrates the importance of the subject now considered. To them, and to all seekers after the truth, I commend what is here offered : to Professors Green and Harper, Bissell and Briggs, Cave and Cheyne, Dods and Driver, and all other Bible students. While I presume not to instruct them, I may suggest that the more they yield to negative criticism, the greater is the danger to be apprehended from it. Though the old traditions may be wrong, they do not err in implying a very ancient date for the Writers of Genesis, and an early writer of Isaiah 40–66.

My suggestions of authorship are not based on Astruc, who died in 1766. He was a physician, not a Bible expositor. That his theory should form the basis of so much modern criticism surprises me. "God is His own Interpreter" of Revelation and of Creation. The discoveries and decipherments of our generation supply abundant reasons for believing that four or five early patriarchs wrote their own memoirs. These were incorporated into our Genesis by Moses, and later prophets explained names of persons and places.

This idea I have worked out by careful analysis and examination of various facts brought to light by the Egypt Exploration Fund and other Oriental societies. Professor Sayce corrects Renan. The literatures of the oldest nations sustain my view; a decent respect for the opinions of mankind supports it; the culture and good sense of the covenant-patriarchs support it. It honors Inspiration and God, the Revealer.

The essay on the Scientific Method Applied to the Bible is the outcome of reading Mr. John Burroughs's article in a late *North American Review;* Babylonians and Egyptians, not Totemists, was evoked by recent lectures under the auspices of Columbia College, and by W. Robertson Smith; Hebrew and Greek Ethics was to correct Mr. Gladstone's third paper upon Holy Scripture. If my aim has been high, I trust I have been enabled to reach the mark.

May the Enlightening Spirit guide us all unto a right conclusion. THE AUTHOR.

CONTENTS.

		PAGE
I. The Writers of Genesis		9
§ 1.	What we Seek	9
§ 2.	What we Find	11
§ 3.	Abraham Distinguishes Jehovah from the God of Melchizedek	16
§ 4.	New Testament Authority	19
§ 5.	Writing in the Fourth Millennium B. C.	29
§ 6.	Knowledge at the Time of the Deluge	38
§ 7.	In Egypt and Babylonia	43
§ 8.	The Tower of Babel	50
§ 9.	Summary of Points	51
§ 10.	Memoirs of Abraham	56
§ 11.	Destruction of Sodom in Accadian Legends	64
§ 12.	Some Domestic Events	67
§ 13.	Memoirs of Isaac	74
§ 14.	Jacob's Memoirs	81
§ 15.	Memoirs of Judah	88
§ 16.	Conclusion	96
II. The Writer of Isaiah 40 to 66		103
III. The Scientific Method Applied to the Bible		139
IV. Ancient Babylonians and Egyptians not Totemists		168
V. Mr. Gladstone on Hebrew and Greek Ethics		180

THE WRITERS OF GENESIS

AND

RELATED TOPICS.

I.

THE WRITERS OF GENESIS.

SECTION I.—*What we seek.*

I SHALL endeavor in these pages to put the average reader in possession of the facts and methods whereby he can determine who were the probable writers of the first book of the Bible. Men now talk learnedly about the Hexateuch, thus massing together that they may afterward pulverize the first six books of Holy Scripture. But it is of chief importance to know if there were not a Primus or First Book, before the redaction of what Moses revised.

Our investigation proposes to show that there was a Primer which Abraham learned, and later prefixed to his Memoirs; and that these Memoirs were continued by Isaac, Jacob, and Judah. From them we obtain the substance of our Genesis; so, even after the revision by Moses, may be discovered differences of style in those early writers.

Thus we may learn whence arose those distinctions in the use of certain names for the Deity, which no late writer would have observed, but which indicate a contemporaneous writing. Thus, too, primitive names of places occur here and there, which were subsequently changed to later ones. If we are charged with instructing our teachers, who are more learned than ourselves in such matters, we may answer, that is only what scholars often do who do their teachers honor.

Indeed, all that may be adduced in favor of Moses being the original writer of Genesis, or of its being the work of several writers and redactors according to the critics, may be said in favor of the authorship herein suggested. Abraham certainly, if not Noah, wrote the memoirs of his times; while those who followed him added to and revised to date under the guidance and revelation of God. This largely accounts for the differences in style and treatment which now puzzle the critics. It is the key which unlocks the mystery of the authorship of Genesis.

"No other book in existence of such varied styles, composed by so many hands, and occupying so long a period in its compilation is marked by so marvellous a unity. A single great scheme underlies, traverses, and interpenetrates the Bible, a great and connected system of truth, as bone and cartilage the human frame; a single, high, gracious and inflexible aim pervades this majestic volume from end to end. In principle and essence the faith of David and Paul, Daniel and John, Abraham and Peter is but one. Genesis and Revelation greet each other across the gulf of ages. God's word is a unit."—*Rev. William T. Sabine.*

"This sacred story, even without the assured and solemn authority which it derives from the inspired character of the Book in which it is found, should always form in sound criticism the base of all history; for considered from a merely human point of view, it contains the most ancient tradition as to the first days of the human race, the only one which has not been disfigured by the introduction of fantastic myths of disordered imagination run wild."—*M. Lenormant.*

The seeming purpose of its first chapters was to instruct man as to the process and Agent in Creation, so as to induce him to serve the God who made him, and to regard His saving methods. Though evidence is wanting that such an account was vouchsafed to the first men, Noah was fairly and Abraham more fully instructed in the origin of things and in Divine revelations. He by the inspiration of God was enabled to correct prevailing errors. Yet it was not given him to teach the absolute and ultimate truth, but what was fundamental touching matter and Spirit.

§ II.— *What we find.*

Thus we find that Genesis was not written to teach modern geology; for the people to whom it was given would not have understood a scientific treatise. But the Creation account in Genesis was to set forth *who was the Author* of the Cosmos, rather than the precise order and method of it. As St. John says, "Without Him was not anything made that had been made." In other words, all material and animal existences were by the creative power of God.

The record is somewhat complex, yet brief. It at once meets and corrects the old Accadian and Zoroastrian ideas and legends of the origin of the Cosmos. Neither Tiamat nor Ahriman, as independent creative powers, had any part in the creation of the universe. There is just enough of detail recorded to remove current errors and to present God as the Creator and Upholder of all worlds and of all existences. The account of creation was to disclose the Creator.

The earth was before those who lived upon it. Darkness was before the light and the sun was before the moon, but both were by the Supreme Being who separated between the day and the night. Light and darkness, angels and archangels, good spirits and those who became evil spirits, were the creation of God. His work was perfect, "excellent." Why, then, Abraham might say to the men of Ur, do you worship the Moon God, or any created objects? and to the men of Larsa, Why do you worship the Sun God, or any powers of nature? Jehovah Elohim was the Creator of matter and spirit, of the sun and the moon. Him alone should men worship, who is above all and who created all. Simply and chiefly to teach these two grand but elementary facts was the creation account in Genesis given to man. We are apt to impose too much upon it.

"The history of the creation in Genesis is not merely a cosmogonic account of primitive date, but above all else it is an express counter statement opposed to the conceptions of Egypt and of Babylon." Von Ranke attributes this to Moses at Sinai, "which no terrestrial vicissitudes have ever touched, and where nothing interposes between God and the world." How, then, could Moses have had any knowledge of the Babylonian conception of the Cosmos? But the universe, according to Mr. H. Spencer's sesquipedalian definition, is the outcome of "a change from an indefinite, incoherent homogeneity to a definite, coherent heterogeneity through continuous differentiations and integrations." Whereupon says Mr. Goldwin Smith, "This universe may well have heaved a sigh of relief when, through the cerebration of an eminent thinker, it had been delivered of this account of its origin."

The second chapter sets forth the institution of the Sabbath, describes the abode of man upon his creation, his conscious superiority to the creatures about him, and how God made woman to be his helper and companion in life. The two were not an outgrowth or development from other creatures, but the creation of God, who brought them together and blessed them. They were to replenish the earth.

Genesis 2 : 15-25 relate how, after the creation of man, he was put in the Garden of Eden to dress and to keep it. This, of course, implies the impartation of needful instruction to him. Large liberty was allowed him, and only one prohibition was imposed: he must not eat of the tree of knowledge of good and evil. Abraham was familiar with such legends, and that man was divinely instructed as to his duty.

Adam was also tested whether he was capable of choosing a companion from among all the creatures to whom he gave names; the choice and the naming suggest considerable intelligence. But Adam did not find an "answering" companion in all the living beings which passed before him. No female gorilla or chimpanzee would please his fancy.

Who but an anti-evolutionist could write the account of the creation of woman at that time? She is made for man, and brought to him as his helpmeet in life. He was an intelligent observer of much that passed, and there was no "almost a woman" among the creatures he had named. He had skill, order, and analysis. He may even have learned to write the account of his education and of Eve's creation before he died. Quite likely it was written before the Deluge, and preserved to the times of Abraham, or of the legends of Ur. They at least taught that God was the Creator and Instructor of man, and that he had sinned against Him. Of how they worshipped Him, the great temple at Ur to the Moon God bore witness. See "Chaldean Account in Genesis," Sayce's "Hibbert Lectures" and Dr. Cave's "Inspiration of the Old Testament."

If we regard the first chapters of Genesis as the Inspired account to Abraham rather than a revelation to Moses, we find it just such a version as a man in that age would give to the people of his day and to those who followed him. But to make it a Revelation to Moses three thousand years after the creation of man, and for the science of the nineteenth century, is to put a meaning upon the record which was not intended when first communicated.

"Science," says Professor J. D. Dana, has made no real progress toward proving that the Divine act was not required for the creation of Man. No remains of ancient Man have been found that indicate a progenitor of lower grade than the lowest of existing tribes; none that show any less of the erect posture and other essential characteristics of the exalted species. Made in the image of God, Man was capable of moral distinctions and of spiritual progress; and hence with him began a new era in history," viz., human accountability and immortality for the crowning work of creation. Surely being made in the image of God implies eternal existence?—*O. and N. Test. Student* for August, 1890, pp. 94, 95.

Chapter third relates how man sinned, the penalty inflicted, how a Redeemer was promised, and the expulsion from Eden. That this account was revealed to Abraham may be inferred from the corrections of prevailing errors. Not in Noah's time had the Babylonians come to speak of Merodach as their Saviour, nor had the men of Ur and of Larsa become worshippers of the heavenly bodies. But they each were this respectively when Abraham was called out of Chaldea. Thus a revelation of what was to come and of what men ought to do was given for instruction in righteousness as well as in knowledge. The account suffers greatly by being relegated to the time of Moses. To Abraham it was disclosed how man had failed in his first trial in Eden, and in his longer trial in the world before the deluge. He was himself a witness of the idolatry in his day among the peoples about the Euphrates. Merodach had failed to save the Babylonians; Osiris had failed to save the Egyptians, and Sosiosh had failed to save the Iranians. Thus the supposed saviours of Hamites, of Semites, and of Aryans had alike failed in saving those representative peoples.

Wherefore the Creator of all chose Abraham to found a new family for the preservation of the true religion among men, and to prepare the world for the Advent of its Redeemer. To Abraham also it was given to understand *why* he was thus chosen, and the *right* of Him who had chosen him. Such a revelation was needed for his instruction and future guidance. So in Canaan and in Egypt he never fell into idolatry, and in Gen. 14 : 19-22 he finely distinguishes between Melchizedek's "God Most High" and "Jehovah, God Most High." It appears in the Revised Version, and marks the difference between the Covenant God of the chosen people and the god or gods of the Gentiles.

§ III.—*Abraham distinguishes Jehovah from the God of Melchizedek.*

We need not go further than Gen. 14 to learn that it was not originally written by Moses. Melchizedek said, "Blessed be God Most High, which hath delivered thine enemies into thy hand." "And Abram said to the king of Sodom, I have lift up mine hand unto the *Lord*, God Most High, possessor of heaven and earth" (verses 20 and 22 of Revised Version). To suppose that the nice distinction of adding Jehovah, the Lord, to the name of Melchizedek's God, to designate the God of Abraham, would have been handed down orally for five or six hundred years without understanding the strong reason for it, or to suppose that it was all revealed to Moses together with all other instances of Divine revelations and religious distinctions, amid the deserts of Sinai, is to my mind the top of folly and critical indiscretion.

I invite the proof that the writer of Ex. 6 : 2-4 was the writer of Gen. 14 : 20, 22. He must have been nodding! And the difficulty here arising, I explain thus : Abraham and his fathers for the first sixty years of his life were worshippers of the heavenly bodies. Joshua 24 : 2 decides this as well as contemporary history, " Beyond the River, your fathers served other gods." Now make the pronoun " them" in Ex. 6 : 3 refer to those fathers and to Abraham during the first sixty years of his life, and it is literally true that none of them knew their God or gods by the name of Jehovah. Even to Isaac and Jacob new revelations of Him were given at the Mount of Sacrifice and at the flight of Jacob. The narrative implies that neither of them had clear ideas of Jehovah till He more fully revealed Himself. See this in Gen. 22 : 1-9, and note the recurrence of Jehovah in verses 11-18.

Moreover, it was not the purpose of Exodus to trace the progress and unfold the methods of revelation. Some matters once known had become forgotten in large measure ; and Abraham and his sons may never have understood the full import of the Divine name when disclosed to them at the first. With all his knowledge, even Moses did not know it. Thus he saw the similarity of his position with that of his forefathers in this respect.

Of the many expositions of these passages, that now offered satisfies the requirements of the text and the judgment of the writer. It is conclusive of different writers, and the critics claim a high antiquity for Gen. 14. It was not orally transmitted during several centuries, nor was it a new revelation to Moses ; but it was written by Abraham. He certainly had no motive to misstate anything in writing his memoirs. Little by little he received Divine revelations in Palestine, but he had lived there twenty-four years before he received circumcision, and he knew not what next would be required. It proved to be the promise of Isaac, and the relief of Lot in Sodom. There was nothing like the development of a theory of religion, but it mostly pertained to family affairs, and needed only a truthful scribe. Its slow growth marks the unfolding of revelation to Abraham.

Professor W. W. Martin's is a striking illustration

of a criticism which overlooks the point to be observed. He appears not to see that Abram's God was all that Melchizedek and the king of Sodom recognized, and as much more as was implied by the addition of the name Jehovah by Abram, *Jahveh*, the ever-living God Most High. So, later in the records, Joseph realized that Jahveh was his Protector, Guide, and Deliverer; yet when he was approached by a wanton woman he reminds her of her God, El or Ra, whom she acknowledged; but not of his covenant Jahveh. As well say that Joseph then denied Him, as that Abram was in danger of making such a denial. (See *Old and New Testament Student* for July, 1890, pp. 46, 47.)

§ IV.—*New Testament Authority.*

We have also a New Testament reason for our suggestion of early patriarchal memoirs. Thus St. Stephen explicitly told his hearers that Moses supposed that his brethren understood how that God by his hand was giving them deliverance (Acts 7 : 25, Revised Version). Add to this what Moses said of himself, that when he was grown up he visited his brethren, looked on their burdens, and smote the Egyptian who was smiting a Hebrew. Again he went out, and behold two men of the Hebrews strove together: and he said to him that did the wrong, Wherefore smitest thou thy fellow? And he said, Who made thee a prince and a judge over us? thinkest thou to kill me, as thou killedst the

Egyptian? And Moses feared, for Pharaoh sought to slay him, and he fled from his face, and dwelt in the land of Midian. In other words, rejected by his own kinsmen and pursued by Pharaoh, he fled to the descendants of Abraham in the desert (Ex. 2 : 11-15).

He had been instructed in the learning of Egypt, of which his brethren knew little, and knew but little of their family and tribal history, nor that Jehovah had promised Abraham to bring them out of that land, with great substance (Gen. 15 : 14). But Moses had learned all this. Readers of the Speaker's and other late commentaries, as well as recent lectures on Egypt, know somewhat of its arts and its literature, and are prepared to follow us in asking, Why did Moses suppose that his brethren understood that God would deliver them by him? The records of his life do not inform us how he learned the history of his own people. Not even his Hebrew mother and elder sister could have taught him all those ancient documents, many of which had become very scarce after those centuries in Egypt. And it is too much to assume that he found the history of Israel among its literature.

In the "Tale of the Two Brothers" he saw a version of the story of Joseph, and he may also have learned other details of the family of Jacob. Indeed, he may have read in Egyptian records an account of the visit of Abraham six or seven centuries before, and a list of the presents made him by the reigning

Pharaoh. But it contained no word for him about Jehovah's covenant with the patriarch, nor about his being the chosen one of God to found a new nation which should prepare for the Messiah, nor that the predicted four hundred years had well-nigh passed, when Israel was to return to Caanan (Gen. 15 : 16).

Yet St. Stephen, who evidently spoke by Divine inspiration, clearly states that Moses *supposed* that God by his hand would deliver Israel. And it may have been the knowledge he had which prompted him to act precipitately in smiting that Egyptian. Moreover, if the tradition of his success as an Egyptian general going against her enemies were true, if the princess who had rescued him were dead, if a Pharaoh like Rameses II. was on the throne, who was jealous of Moses, a man of leisure and of influence about the court, then these were other reasons which might have led him to suppose that he was the one to deliver his countrymen, and lead them to the land of their fathers. But success under such conditions would have given a secular aspect to the Exodus, leaving no play for the Divine in the passage of the Red Sea, nor for the giving of the Law at Sinai. So his first attempt failed.

Let us put ourselves in Moses's place. With all his knowledge of Egyptian literature, what could he know of the God of the Hebrews who had covenanted with Abraham? What could he know of the most important parts of his people's history?

He was forty years old. He had not learned the lessons of the Desert, nor the lessons which Jethro taught him, nor the legends and traditions of the Midianites. But he was a man of intellectual activity and capacity. In what, during the ten years of his life from thirty to forty, was he occupied? St. Stephen's words must be remembered and accounted for. *Moses supposed* that *his brethren understood* (we must trace up the grounds for that supposition and understanding) how that God by his hand was giving them deliverance; but their conduct showed that they understood not. Prophets had not arisen to tell them, and *Moses himself had not then received his commission, nor been vouchsafed a Revelation to teach them ;* and he anticipated the time and mistook the methods for the deliverance of his brethren from Egypt. But he had learned some things which were suggestive.

How had Moses learned the history of his people, whereby he could be led into such a supposition? For, according to the critical view, and even according to the traditional view of Genesis, this book was *not* then written. Did Moses, before the act which precipitated his flight, receive the patriarchal history which induced him to form his supposition from the direct inspiration of God—his precipitate conduct notwithstanding—or did he learn that history from the family records of the Hebrews? In other words, was the Book of Genesis a Revelation to Moses, or were the patriarchal portions of it family records made at the time of the events narrated? Were the Divine voices, visions, and promises recorded when first vouchsafed to man, or were they all left to be revealed a second time from God?

Consider the *supposition* of Moses before his commission; consider that only one preacher of warning was given to the antediluvians; that only one grand pleading for Sodom is preserved to us; that only one prophet was sent to warn Nineveh, though other prophetic messages were sent; that no new Table of the Law was made for the new Temple at Jerusalem after the return from exile; that no substitute for Divine worship was provided for the Ten Tribes after the disruption by Jeroboam, notwithstanding the apostasy which followed. So no *new* Revelation was made to the compiler of Genesis at the close of the patriarchal records which ended with the death and embalming of Joseph in Egypt.

From Abraham to Moses was about six hundred years. During that time revelations were made from God, which were not repeated as revelations, for they had been carefully preserved in the Hebrew records, and only needed a correct copyist or an inspired commentator. Such copyist they had in Egypt, and Moses had obtained copies of those records by purchase long before his flight; and he became an inspired commentator of them while in Midian, having been a diligent student of them. From such study he came to form the supposition which St. Stephen attributed to him—*i.e.*, from the study of the records of the patriarchs.

My belief is, and I shall endeavor to show, that Noah, Abraham, Isaac, Jacob, Judah, and Joseph were the original writers of those portions of Genesis in which they appear as the active subjects. And it matters not upon this method of treatment who was the first redactor, according to the critics, nor whether E or J or P or R find any place in the early or late editions of the Book. But my treatment will assign to Moses the first editing of the records of Judah, which ended with the death of Joseph. In Egypt and in Midian he collected all the Hebrew records and traditions. They had kindled his enthusiasm and incited him to undue haste, when he slew the offending Egyptian. It was the outcome of the first active decade of his life. Then, with his literary treasures, he escaped from an indignant and angry court.

We may believe that Rameses II. was the Pharaoh at this time, and was not disposed to look lightly on such an offence as that which Moses had committed. And the hiding the body of the Egyptian in the sand, where it was not to be seen, embalmed, and buried, was to deprive the dead of immortality. For however just his soul may have been, yet without his body, which could be preserved for three thousand years only by embalming, the Egyptian supposed immortality to be impossible. It aggravated the crime. The rage of Rameses II. against the Hyksos incited him to obliterate every trace of them from the region they had occupied for centuries. And M. Maspero has shown us the sculptures from which he had erased the Hyksos legends and inscribed those of himself instead. This alone is strong proof against the rhetoric of Renan, that the Hyksos were permitted to remain in Egypt and to fight the battles of the Hebrews in their oppression! No; not even Moses himself felt safe till he had fled to the desert of Midian. There he married the daughter of the priest-king; there he learned other details and traditions of that branch of Abraham's descendants, and there, during his forty years' exile, he worked over and arranged for the Hebrew people the Book of Genesis as preserved to us, from the earlier writings of the patriarchs. But he attempted no account of the residence in Egypt.

He was a learned man, an active man, a born leader of his people. His character when he fled from Pharaoh Rameses II. became more mature and ripe, and was permeated with the Divine Spirit when he returned and stood before Pharaoh Menephtah, saying, "Thus saith Jehovah, let my people Israel go, that they may hold a feast unto Me in the wilderness." It was not an unknown region, but the country from which the now duly commissioned leader had just returned after a memorable interview with the God of Abraham, and where for ages the Egyptians had mines which they worked.

2

Such a man as that could not be content with tending sheep for his father-in-law. His mind brooded over the past, over his former opportunity and mistakes, over the possibilities of the future; and he was inspired by Jehovah to do His bidding. The time had now come. Rameses II., the powerful king, had died, and Menephtah reigned in his stead. Such are some of the well-attested facts of Moses's life and times. He personally was not a miracle, but, with the rod of God, was a worker of miracles. Like Elijah in a later age, he was human, fed by daily food to nourish his body, and his soul was sustained by the Divine Spirit, while his mind was full of the history and appointed destiny of Israel. He knew that covenant promise in Gen. 15 : 13–18; that his people had been strangers and servants in Egypt for four hundred years; that their oppressors were about to be judged, and that Israel should go forth with great substance. A mother's love had saved him for a great mission. A father's knowledge had been imparted to him. Family affection, the watchfulness of Miriam, the prophetic eloquence of Aaron, cherished him and centred around him. Thus Moses was instructed in Hebrew traditions as well as in Egyptian learning.

Critics in various analyses and books upon Genesis object to the traditional views of its authorship. They claim to find diversity in style and treatment; that some words are peculiar to each writer, especially the names for Deity, etc. Be it so. My suggestion of the patriarchal origin and writing of the first book of the Bible fully accounts for all existing differences of style and of verbal characteristics. I shall waste no words upon the orthography, syntax, or grammar of the writers. Possibly some of them never learned to conjugate a Hebrew verb. They have been described as writing in a style now free and flowing, now concise and rigid, now using stories and traditions, now picturesque, poetical, prophetic in their delineations. And if we allow several writers and revisers of the first nine chapters, followed by Abraham for his portion, by Isaac for his register, by Jacob for his records and visions, by Judah for the continuance and completion of the history and of the story of Joseph, and by Moses as the inspired redactor and reviser of the whole into what is substantially our present Book of Genesis, we shall find ample room for verbal variations in sections, for differences in style, for some explanatory words and sentences, while all is duly authenticated. It was a progressive writing during seven hundred years.

I am quite aware that such a suggestion, if made thirty years ago, would have been regarded as absurd, having no grounds to rest upon. Indeed, when a youth I maintained the affirmative in more than one discussion of the question whether *Moses* could write! Now, however, my theme requires probable proof and illustration that Abraham could write; that Isaac could write his treaty with Abimelech, for example; that Jacob recorded his visions at Beth-el and Peniel; and that Judah of the signet ring was the Scribe of his people. The method must be largely inductive. However, I shall first state the reasons and grounds on which my suggestion is based.

The point at which we start and to which we must return is the probability that Abraham could read and write. Modern research has discovered the temple in which he worshipped, the name of the god he adored, and the Psalm of adoration which for forty years he chanted. The temple was that of Sin, the male moongod of Ur, and the prayer psalm is not only devout, but it suggests the style of some theological parts of Genesis; and that the man who early learned that prayer was the writer of certain Divine names.

We also find on the bricks of the lower stage of the great temple the inscribed name of King Urukh or Ligbagas who built it. He also built the wall of Ur. It was the most ancient capital of Accad, and was a sacred city distinguished for its learning. This hymn to its patron deity was written in Accadian and Assyrian, on a tablet now in the British Museum. I give part of it, as rendered in Tomkins's "Times of Abraham." Professor Sayce translates it in the "Hibbert Lectures" for 1887. We may imagine Abraham singing:

"Lord! prince of gods of heaven and earth, whose mandate is exalted!

Father! god enlightening earth! Lord! good god, of gods the prince!
Father! god enlightening earth! Lord! great god, of gods the prince!
Father! god enlightening earth! Lord god of the month, of gods the prince!
Father! god enlightening earth! Lord of Ur, of gods the prince!
Father mine, of life the giver, cherishing, beholding all!
Lord, who power benign extendeth over all the heaven and earth!
Seasons, rains, from heaven forth-drawing, watching life and yielding showers!
Father, long-suffering in waiting, whose hand upholds the life of mankind.
Thou thy will in heaven revealest; thee celestial spirits praise!"

§ V.— *Writing in the fourth millennium B. C.*

While I hold that certain dynasties of Egypt and that certain kings of Babylonia were contemporaneous, I am free to admit the great antiquity of reading and writing in those lands. Professor Maspero says : " Hebron no doubt was acquainted with the Hittite writing of Zoan, adopted it, and possessed writings from a remote date." (See " Bible Growth and Religion," pp. 87–90.) Abraham came from Ur, which was even then a centre of learning. Sargon I. may have been before him, and certainly was not long after him. A copy of his annals has come down to us. He was a successful general and organizer, and a collector of libraries which made him famous. He traversed and conquered the countries north and west to Cyprus, and on its rocks he inscribed a likeness of himself. He also carried large booty from that island to Asia. Other inscribed figures of that era have been found. Indeed, Sargon I. dedicated an inscribed egg of veined marble to the Sun God of Sippara, which is now in the British Museum ; and the seal of his librarian, Ibni-sarru, is in the hands of M. Le Clercq, of Paris. There is an ancient tradition and legend of him as Sargina, who was preserved and rescued in a way similar to that of Moses in Egypt. The pyramid builders were as early as the fourth millennium B.C., when the Babylonians had their quarries in Sinai, and from thence transported blocks of stone to Babylonia. All which are evidences of art and culture at that time. And when Khammuragas reigned, about 2300 B.C., there seems to have been a great literary revival, when the main bulk of Accadian literature came into existence. (Sayce's "Hibbert Lectures" for 1887, pp. 29–33 and 420.)

"On the rocks of Wady Magharah, in the Sinaitic peninsula, may be seen to this day an incised tablet representing Sneferu, the first monarch of the fourth dynasty, in the act of smiting an enemy, whom he holds by the hair of his head. At the side we may see the words, *Ta satu*, Smiter of the nations." A famous second dynasty tablet is in the Ashmolean Museum at Oxford. There are other inscriptions of an early age.

Mr. Theodore G. Pinches, in a letter to the *Academy* of January 21st, 1888, and to the English editor of Schrader's "Cuneiform Inscriptions," vol. 2, which that editor incorporated into it, says that one of the tablets of Babylonian inscriptions of about 3000 B.C. may be thus rendered: "The day for the worship of the gods was the delight of his (the writer's) heart, and the prayer of a king—that was joy. How did he learn the path of God glorious, who in the world lived, died, renewed? . . . Open the high place, they have granted my prayer (?), until there be no more death, and weeping cease." This inscription was considered so important as very early to be accompanied with a glossary to explain all the hard and obsolete words in the ancient text. Again and again the copyist wrote, "How has he learned the path of God glorious, who in the world lived, died, renewed?" Moreover, the office of Mediator was anciently performed by Marduk, probably referring to the "One who in the world lived, died, renewed." It is a Messianic prophecy, which possibly found fulfilment in Marduk 3000 years B.C. And writing was then known in Babylonia and in Egypt.

For confirmation let us turn to Gen. 4 : 19-22, where we read of Jabal, the father of such as dwell in tents—tents which imply spinning and weaving. Jabal's brother was Jubal of the harp and organ or pipe, implying yet more skill than tent-making. Then we have Tubal-Cain, the forger of every cutting instrument of brass or copper and iron. And this stage of art and mechanics was before the death of Adam. No rearrangement of the records would place this item after the father of Noah.

In the *Babylonian and Oriental Record* for January, 1890, Mr. Pinches recounts sundry traditions of the Chinese, such as those of the Deluge, Creation, Paradise, the Tree of Knowledge, the Temptation, the Fall, the Curse, traditions of Satan and the Angels, and of the Dispersion of mankind.

In the creation of Adam they say, " Father God took a piece of His life, and breathed into the nostrils of the man and the woman He had created, and they were real human beings. Thus creation was finished." In a series of papers in that journal it is shown that the Chinese may be traced back to the reign of Khammuragas in Babylonia, whence they emigrated, about 2300 B.C. His reign of fifty-five years is identified with that of Belos, who is also identified with Bel-Merodach (pp. 16, 19, 22).

In the Chaldean legend preserved by Berosus we are told that Xisuthros—another name for Noah—was commanded, just before the Deluge, to bury all written documents known to him at Sippara, the ancient book town near Babylon. This he did, and upon leaving the Ark after the flood he returned to Sippara, disinterred those buried treasures, and thus transmitted them to posterity. Hence the written knowledge of the antediluvians has come down to us. However that may be, we find a close resemblance in the ideas, thoughts, and legends of primitive man wherever scattered.

Old Sippara and Agâde, near by, were probably the "Sepharvaim" of the Book of Kings and of Isaiah. The spade and modern decipherments have disclosed their long-buried inscriptions, so that to-day we have much of their learning. The writings of old Accad, Babylon, and Egypt have been translated into modern tongues. If we have not yet learned the processes of their thought, we have abundant evidences of their writing, their art, and mechanical skill. These clearly express their ideas of creation and of Providence, how man came into being, how God was the directive Force in the ordering of the world, how He was worshipped in the first ages, and how He communicated His will to man. Sometimes their ideas are crude and mythical, and sometimes they mistake the order of nature. Thus Accadian legends place the Moon before the creation of the Sun, and they give the woman precedence over the man; they also give a polytheistic coloring to their Deluge legends, and express providential oversight by making the planets "gods of the sky," who, dwelling in them, kept them from going wrong.

If Genesis tells how God placed at the entrance to Eden, after man's expulsion, cherubim and a flaming sword which turned every way, to keep the way to the Tree of Life, the Gizdhubar- legends tell of

"The scorpion men who guard its gate,
   Of whom consuming is their terribleness, and their aspect death,
   Great is their majesty, o'ershadowing the forests.
   At the rising of the Sun and the setting of the Sun they guard the Sun."

In other words—so Mr. St. Boscawen, in the June number of the *Babylonian and Oriental Record* for 1889—Gizdhubar encounters " certain strange Cherubim-like guardians of the gates of the Sun, described as scorpion men, whose heads tower to the dome of Heaven, and whose feet rest in the shadow of the land, or house of death. In their appearance they are terrible, burning, consuming, as the flaming sword was of the Hebrew Scriptures. Beyond them, moreover, it is said (in col. 5), lay a beautiful garden which they guarded, further characterized as being ' equal to the trees of the gods in aspect,' ' bearing emeralds as its fruit,' ' whose branches bend not to uphold the crystal covering they bear as foliage,' ' pleasant to the sight.' This last phrase, it is needless to add, recalls that portion of the description of the biblical garden :

"' Every tree that is pleasant to sight and good for food ' (Gen. 2 : 9).

"The scorpion-men of this legend serve, like the guardians of Eden, to exclude the hero, Gizdhubar, from access to this paradisaical garden, and from the Tree of Life, where he might restore his sick and declining frame."

Moreover, a cylinder of hard stone, now in the

British Museum, has a tree represented on it with several horizontal branches on either side ; the lowest branches bear, each, a large bunch of fruit. A man sits on one side of the tree and a woman on the other side. They stretch out their hands as if to pluck the fruit. Behind the woman stands a serpent erect (Smith's " Chaldean Account in Genesis," pp. 88-91). These two records of the tablets can mean nothing less than the Fall and expulsion of Man from Eden. They inform us of the temptation and of the punishment of man.

Following upon that first sin is a legend in different versions of Cain and Abel. As was quite natural, Mother Eve was early regarded as the daughter of God, for so indeed she was by creation. The birth of her first child was a real astonishment. No wonder she came to be considered as a goddess, offspring of the Great God. Very early the evening star was made her symbol, and then the morning star. First deified as Nana, 2500 years B.C. or sooner, she was then called Istar. Her image, carried off 1635 years before Assur-bani-pal, was recovered by his generals at the capture of Shushan. She was long the supposed bride of Tammuz, the goddess of Assur and of Babylonia. At first pure as heaven, she was then debased to earth, and made the innocent patron of licentiousness.

Her legend in the Gizdhubar Epic may have incorporated somewhat of the story of Nimrod and of the older tragedy of Cain, who slew his brother.

For, instead of being the bride of Tammuz, she was, in fact, his mother, who mourned for her son when slain by his brother Adar. Such was the Accadian version of Cain and Abel. We can form little conception of the astonishment at the first human birth; greater yet was that at the first death. Terrible indeed was the horror of the first murder. The amazement and anguish of Eve at the lifeless body of her son cannot be expressed in words. Sculpture and the painter can better do it. See the striking attempt in a group in the Metropolitan Museum, and also the horrible expression of the Cain. We quote Byron as he makes Mother Eve exclaim:

"May the grass wither from thy feet! the woods
Deny thee shelter! earth a home! the dust
A grave! the sun his light, and heaven her God!"

Some such feeling and sympathy with the first mother prompted, we may believe, the daughters of Babylonia to make annual lamentation for the dead Tammuz, which is but another name for Abel. Hence the origin of that ancient custom and of portions of the old Babylonian epic, which is far more a tragedy than a love story. Like Rachel weeping for her children, the mother of Tammuz and her daughters wept for their dead. It was Eve who became the goddess Istar; the first of deified humanity, and the longest to retain her hold upon man. Thus motherhood was early honored in our world by practices which degenerated into base superstitions. As the Venus God, Istar was worshipped at

Accad, Erech, Sippara, Ur, and Haran in the era of Abraham; as Ashtoreth and Astarte by the Phœnicians, and as Diana and Venus by Greeks and Romans. The murder of Tammuz was thought to have been avenged in the Deluge of Noah.

Genesis was the first Hebrew book of science, the first Hebrew history, and the first book of theology. And it was in advance of any other science or history which has come down to us. In other words, the science disclosed in our Bible and the history recorded therein are in advance of all other writings of the earliest ages. It must, therefore, have had an inspired author. Abraham probably rewrote the first nine chapters of Genesis, compiled from still earlier records; but if they were first written by Moses, the marvel is great; for it required a *revelation of past events* as well as of the creation story.

Besides an account of the Sacred Tree, the Serpent, and the Expulsion for the sin of man, found in various ethnic traditions, Genesis gives an account of the *unity* of the human race, which is sustained by Baron Cuvier, by Dr. Prichard, and by Quartrefages. Even Darwin was a monogenist. Then we have the unity of language as stated in Genesis confirmed by modern analysis. Max Müller reduces the entire speech of man to about one hundred and twenty roots, or mother ideas. Every thought that ever crossed the mind of man can be traced back to about one hundred and twenty simple concepts ("Science of Thought"). Man's bodily structure, his instincts, senses, appetites, affections, mental faculties, religious capacities—all point to the same ethnic origin. As to color, the Jew is white in England and America, brown in Italy, olive in Syria, coffee-colored in Arabia, and almost black in Abyssinia. Touching religion, man is everywhere religious, even to superstition. He prays as naturally as he laughs. So in all these grand tests of truthfulness our Genesis is indisputably true. The ethnography of chapter 10 is true history, though, perhaps, written after the birth of Moab and Ammon, if not of Ishmael and Esau. From the sons of Noah the world has been peopled. Upon these several matters are some excellent remarks by Dr. A. Cave in his "Inspiration of the Old Testament," pp. 110-160. Whatever knowledge of these things Abraham got from current legends and traditions, the arrangement and revision of them, if used in compiling our Genesis, *required Divine Inspiration.*

§ VI.—*The Deluge and Knowledge then.*

Briefly, we find that God told Noah when to build the Ark; God sent the destruction upon man; shut the door of the Ark; assuaged the flood of waters; set His bow in the heavens in token that He would not again destroy man with a Flood; and when the sweet odors of Noah's sacrifice ascended to the skies, *God* smelled the fragrance. For it is remarkable that while the legends give a polytheistic version of the account, our Genesis corrects them, saying,

"Jehovah"—God in Divine Unity—smelled the sweet savor of that sacrifice. It looks like a record carefully made by the saved man, whose knowledge in other matters doubtless included the ability to write out his wonderful experiences.

Moreover, the legend of the preservation of the antediluvian writings at Sippara can mean nothing less than that, in that far-off age, men were competent to read and write. Even before the Deluge this art was known among men, and so they who lived near that catastrophe believed. Their brick inscriptions inform us how the older written knowledge was preserved. Accadian and Egyptian legends have been discovered and deciphered which make this fact clear. For legend is not a myth or a guess, but a reading, and those ancient legends record impressions of how mankind were preserved from total extinction. In Chaldea, Egypt, India, China, they testify that such preservation was by Divine interposition. Brick, stone, papyrus, are uniform in the main facts. A long-lived race had the time needed for various learning. Step by step they attained to the treasures of knowledge, and they were careful to record for after generations their ideas and achievements. Forgeries no one pretends them to be ; but even forgery would prove a true original. Men do not counterfeit the spurious, but the genuine ; the actual, not the fictitious. To invent Deluge legends is absurd.

Possibly the Egyptian story of Thoth and his

wonderful book, whose contents, even a single page, would charm the heavens and the earth, the seas and the mountains, may have arisen from the legend of the book knowledge of the world preserved at Sippara, notwithstanding the misfortune which it brought upon its possessor. Or it may have been a version of the forbidden knowledge obtained by eating of the forbidden fruit in Eden, which, as in the Pandora's box of the Greeks, brought unspeakable evils upon mankind.

Then their destruction by the God Ra, as told in another Egyptian story, cannot have been without a foundation in truth. "For a long time he had reigned over obedient subjects, but at length they grew headstrong and unruly; they uttered words against Ra; they plotted evil things; they grievously offended him. So he called a council of the celestials to consider what he should do. They advised that mankind be destroyed. Hathor and Sekhet were commissioned to the work of destruction, and proceeded to smite the men over the whole land. This brought fear and repentance upon them, and the men of Elephantine made haste to propitiate the gods. They extracted the juice from the best of their fruits, mingled it with human blood, filled seven thousand jars with it, and brought them as an offering to the Deity. Ra drank and was content, and bade that the liquor which remained be poured out of the jars; when, lo! an inundation covered the whole land of Egypt. And when

Hathor went forth the next day to destroy, she saw no men in the fields, but only water, which she drank; it pleased her, and she went away satisfied." Some, indeed, see no reference to the Deluge in this story, while others of undoubted learning and judgment do. It implies that a destruction had been wrought as a punishment for the sins of men by the Deity, and that those who survived the pestilence or smiting of Hathor were destroyed by inundation of the river. By a confusion in the order of events, the propitiatory sacrifice of the Elephantines, though acceptable to Ra, failed to procure the desired respite. This is unaccountable. In another version of this story, by M. Naville, in "Records of the Past," he represents some men as saved, and that the practice of making libations to Hathor arose from that fact. Lenormant suggests the correspondence of Ra in Egypt with Bel in Chaldea, and that the form of the tradition was changed to suit the feelings of the Egyptians, who regarded the overflowing Nile as a benefaction. Hence the destructive gods were the slayers of men. (See "God in Creation," pp. 101-111.) Such variations in the account are not denials of the catastrophe.

In the Accadian legend the variations are marked. Principal Dawson has called attention to them in a paper in the *Contemporary Review* for December, 1889. There a "steersman" is introduced, the ship is "launched," not floated with the rising waters; while the dimensions of the Ark are largely increased. Its construction and navigation imply advanced knowledge in such matters. The Biblical is the more reasonable account, but that is of a vessel 300 cubits long, 50 cubits wide, and 30 cubits high, with lower, second, and third stories, having sundry compartments. It was to be of such form and strength as to carry an immense cargo of provisions and living animals, endure a terrific downpour from heaven, and withstand the shocks of a breaking up of the foundations of the great deep. That catastrophe included upheavals, convulsions, and various destructive forces at work. The saving vessel must be duly proportioned, well built, and capacious. Nor was it a mere float, but a three-decked vessel as large as an Atlantic steamer. Those 300 cubits were nearly 600 feet, the width was about twice that of a large steamer, and the depth some 55 ft. The sacred cubit is supposed to have been two of our feet, or 25 inches.

While 30 and 50 are factors of 300, few builders would trust their memory with the figures, nor with the deck measurement and divisions of the Ark. Then as now the skill to build such a huge float implies the skill to *write* down the directions. Add to this the legend of the preservation of the ancient writings by burying them at Sippara, and it emphasizes the probability that the antediluvians were able to read and write. In nothing is the testimony of the three great families of man more corroborative than in Deluge legends. See that chapter in

"God in Creation;" in Dr. Cave's "Inspiration of the Bible;" in Dr. Fradenburgh's "Witnesses from the Dust," and in Lenormant's and Sir Principal Dawson's works. Dr. Cave notes that Yima, in the Aryan story, was commanded to build "when six hundred winters" had passed over him, and that "Noah was six hundred years old when the Flood broke." Moreover, the Accadians and Lithuanians confirm Genesis in having the rainbow as the sign of God's returning favor. Sir William Dawson corrects the usually judicious Schrader, who objected to "the omission of the swallow, when the story passed over to the Hebrews. It is one of the most amusing instances of the inversion of sound criticism which results when unscientific commentators tamper with the plain statements of truthful and observant witnesses. The addition of the swallow in the Chaldean version is a mark of interpolation, arising from a local and popular superstition attached to the swallow." Our chief business with these legends now is not confirmation of the fact of the Deluge of Noah, but rather that in his era, before and after, man could probably record such events, and record them correctly.

§ VII.—*In Egypt and Babylonia.*

Amenemhat I., of the twelfth dynasty, wrote detailed "Instructions" to his son—the earliest literary production of royalty that has reached us. Writing, however, was exceeded by the skill which built the great pyramid of Khufu of the fourth dynasty, and the pyramid of Shafra soon after. They are the most ancient remains of those times and reach back to very near the Deluge. What skill in engineering and the mechanic arts is implied to raise such huge blocks of rock, nicely chiselled and fitted into a compact mass, in comparison with which our modern cathedrals are but chapels. If Egyptologists are right in dating them at about 3300 B.C., the skill thus manifested in the morning of the world renders probable the truth of the legend that even before the Deluge men wrote out the events of their times.

Indeed, there are sculptures and inscriptions of Sneferu's officers which prove hieroglyphic and picture writing of before the year 3000 of our era. Earlier still was that second dynasty tablet now in the Ashmolean Museum at Oxford; while the metaphysical distinctions of man made him to consist of body, soul, spirit or intelligence, life, shadow and name; so M. Maspero and others. Miss Edwards adds that "the Book of the Dead shows that all these several parts had to be restored to the man, and reunited before he could obtain immortality." The subtlety of the classification is remarkable for the period. And, says Rawlinson, "No rudeness or want of finish attaches either to the writing or to the drawing of Sneferu's time; the artists do not attempt much, but what they attempt they accomplish." Moreover, at Meydoum and at

Sakkara are pyramids earlier than those of Khufu and Shafra, of whom and of Una we find inscriptions. Then of the eleventh and twelfth dynasties we have a literature.

A tomb of the eleventh dynasty records of the dead reposing within it: "I was beloved by the king more than his nobles and officers in all the South. He caused me to rule when I was a mere child of a cubit high. He elevated my seat when I still wore the lock of youth; he had me taught to swim with the royal children. I was a marvel of uprightness (a servant), who did no injury to his master, who had trained him from a child. Siût was contented with my administration, Heracleopolis Magna praised God for me, Upper and Lower Egypt said, 'This is the wisdom of a great prince.'"

This was in the dynasty before Abraham, when the two Egypts were under one sovereign, and prior to the Hyksos domination.

Another inscription, probably of the tenth dynasty, says of the Prince of Siût: "I came to my city, I entered my nome; I did what men desired, what the gods approved; I gave bread to the hungry, and clothes the naked; I listened to the cry of the widow, I gave a dwelling to the homeless. I returned evil with good, and sought not injury, in order that I might remain long on the earth, and thence pass to perfection." Then a blessing is invoked on his friends. "But every evil one, every perverse one who shall do the reverse of these things which he has heard, his name shall not remain, he shall not be buried in the necropolis-hill, he shall be destroyed with the wicked." See "Report of Egypt Exploration Fund for 1888-89," and other translations in it. These inscriptions fittingly preceded the writing of Genesis, and were not improbably known to Abraham.

Even while revising these pages news comes from England of the receipt of another collection of inscribed tablets which were written at different times from about 2300 to 200 years B.C. in Chaldea. Some of the tablets were enclosed in clay envelopes, on which another copy is written. One such pair dates about 2200 B.C., and discloses the curious fact that thus early agents were employed in Babylon to obtain children for adoption by wealthy citizens who had none of their own. Those agents were paid a regular commission by the parents of such children and by those who adopted them. The humanity thus illustrated is an important feature of the life of those times.

Moreover, we have the mute speaking Sphinx, so wise in his silence, and the Tower of Babel, either of which necessitated a high degree of mechanical skill, not far distant from the era of the Flood. Sippara, on the Euphrates, and Kerioth-sepher, near the Jordan, were book-towns of great antiquity, and possessed a written literature. What is recorded of Noah and his sons, which lifts the veil from his couch and the curtain of his tent, is of a kind to be written, not carried in the memory. They were not revelations to the compiler of Genesis, but were matters of history, of legend and tradition, for the instruction of men, who had not to wait six centuries for them to be written.

The blessing upon Shem and Japheth and the curse of Canaan began to be realized before Israel entered Palestine. Thus the words "Ham was the father of Canaan" have long been regarded as true in application to those doomed tribes who found the avenger of Noah in conquering Joshua. The malediction and its fulfilment, not far apart in our records, were some two thousand years apart in accomplishment. And of those two millenniums Father Abraham learned much of the history from the ancient tablets of Ur and Accad. The language of Babylon, we are now assured, was then the language of commerce and of international communication. By it the lords of Chaldea and the princes of Palestine could readily converse with the princes of Egypt. Nor was Abraham behind them in literary culture. (See "Bible Growth and Religion," pp. 44–61.) He certainly had no difficulty in conversing with Pharaoh Usertesen II., who probably reigned when he fled from the famine of Canaan.

Indeed, the art of writing is traced a thousand years back of Abraham. While Mr. Flinders Petrie describes papyri of the twelfth dynasty, other written papyri of that era have been found in the Fayum excavations. And Professor Sayce writes of an

Egyptian scarab, with its duplicate of the first dynasty. Upon examining it, he found an inscription which he renders, "The Lord of the North and the South, Amu." Amu is a Semitic word, meaning "the terrible one," the plural of which occurs in Gen. 14 : 5; Deut. 2 : 10, 11. There the word designates the Emim, who were then the people of that land, and were so called by the Moabites, who succeeded the Emim in possession of that country. Dr. Naville has also found among the inscriptions of Bubastis the same name, Amu, which may have denoted a god at an early period; but Professor Sayce asks: "Was it the name of an unknown prince?" (The *Academy* for July 20th, 1889, and for October 26th, 1889.) Whatever the word meant, its being inscribed on a scarab of that era proves the remote antiquity of writing, of which the tablets of Tel-el-Amarna furnish additional illustrations. Long before Abraham left Babylonia, and before he visited Egypt, reading and writing were common in both lands. It was the assured way to honor and wealth. Children of nobles, sometimes children of slaves, were taught to read and write. There was no difficulty from lack of the required skill to record the early history of mankind and of God's dealing with them from the days of Seth, when men worshipped Jehovah in public assemblies, to Noah's acceptable sacrifice and Abraham's call out of Ur. Lenormant suggests a series of revelations during that period.

Whatever the method of instruction, the teaching itself was from above, by the Spirit of God. Thus knowledge of Creation, of Paradise almost everywhere found, of Expulsion thence, of a Promised Redeemer, of the Serpent as an evil-worker, of Sabbath and Sacrifice, of Immortality, of good and bad Spirits, and of God's overruling Providence for the benefit of man—these ten elements of religion were very early known, and may be clearly traced among the three great races descended from Noah. This has been done for the general reader in the little book "God Enthroned in Redemption," published by Mr. Whittaker, New York. It is certainly probable that those primitive men recorded and carefully cherished their early knowledge, which was divinely imparted. In no other way can we account for the similarity of thought and action among the scattered nations.

Adam, Noah, and some other names of early patriarchs have not yet been deciphered in Babylonian inscriptions; showing an earlier and independent origin of Bible names which were not derived from them. But we find some names of animals the same in the Bible and in India; viz., those for elephant, ape, peacock; in Egypt, kafi; Sanskrit, kapi; Hebrew, kuf; Greek, kepus; Latin, cepus. So Conder's "Syrian Stone Lore." As it is not pretended that the Hebrews borrowed from the Hindus, such similarity of names would seem traceable to a common origin before separation from the same ancestral home.

§ VIII.—*Tower of Babel.*

Not only does the ethnology of Gen. 10 bear the test of criticism, but we find confirmation of the Tower of Babel and the confusion of tongues in the brick inscriptions. Early fragments of the accounts have been discovered, which accentuates the skill of the first ages. Compare Gen. 11 : 1–9 with the "find" which astonished Mr. George Smith in 1875. Though torn from its connection, it is supposed to have been preceded by another narrative. The fragment is rendered : "Babylon to sin corruptly went ; small and great were mingled on the mound. Make strange their speech ; make hostile their counsel. The King of the holy mound their work confounded. To their stronghold at night they went ; entirely an end he made. In his anger the secret counsel he declared ; to scatter abroad his face was set ; to confuse or make strange their speech (the verb is similar to the Hebrew) he gave command. The builders continued to build ; against the gods they revolted. Even the gods lamented the Babylonians. By whirlwind and storm their work was destroyed." Another fragment reads : "Against the father of all the gods was wickedness . . . and great he confounded their speech. Babylon is brought to subjection." Mr. George Smith also discovered cylinders on which tall piles and the outline of a god were represented. There were figures with outstretched hands resting on tall piles, as if erecting them, and a god is portrayed in the company. The legend is believed to be identical with the account in Genesis.

But, very ancient as is the tradition, it is not alone. When the tablets were well known and one of their two languages was a living tongue, Berosus read it, and incorporated it into his history. He speaks of "earth's first inhabitants who gloried in their strength, despised the gods, and undertook to erect a tower which should reach to the sky. It was on the site where Babylon now stands. But the gods diversified their speech; for till then men spoke the same language. By the winds of Heaven their work was overturned. Whereupon war arose between Kronus or Saturn, and Titan. From the confusion of tongues thence arising, the Hebrews called the place Babel." A similar version by the Sibyl is given in Cory's "Ancient Fragments," p. 75, and see p. 55. There is also a probable reference to the Tower of Babel in the historic account of Nebuchadnezzar's rebuilding the great temple of Bel Merodach. He says "The earthquake and the thunder had dispersed the sun-dried clay. He changed not the site, nor removed the foundation, but set his hand to finish it as it was in former times."

§ IX.—*Summary of Points.*

Thus, in the early records of God in Creation, in similar religious ideas among the representative nations of early ages, in the ethnic history of Genesis, in Deluge legends, tower-building, speech-confounding, and primitive civilization, we have illustrations of culture and education among men; which imply the ability to read and write in the days of Noah; which suggest how Abraham learned the knowledge he possessed, and from his known character as the chosen one to found a new people who should preserve the true religion in the world, mark him out as the *Inspired* collector, reviser, redactor and editor of the first eleven chapters of Genesis. They were written in a form which suited the men of that era, were calculated to further the Divine purposes, and were adapted to the capacity of the young Hebrew people. They were written for a Divine purpose and plan, partly to correct the then polytheistic notions which prevailed in Babylonia and in Egypt, and to teach that God Almighty created the heavens and the earth, and was the Creator and Preserver of mankind. It was not to teach science according to our notions of science, but to teach and to unfold the origin of man, some of the accomplished facts in his past, and some grand facts and developments of his future. Both creation and man—its crowning work—were of God, whose Providence still governed in the affairs of man, and whose educational and uplifting designs were yet to be accomplished in a chosen nation for the Redemption of mankind, and in the final coronation of sanctified humanity.

Hence we name Abraham as the compiler of the first chapters of Genesis, under the Inspiration of God, while those following were from Divine Revelations and personal experiences. Hence we learn the foundation of the *right* and the *why* Jehovah selected a Hebrew family to be His chosen people.

The one objection to this view of the writer of those first chapters is the use of the Divine name Jehovah and compounding it with names of places, as in Moriah, Jehovah-Jireh, and as found in the Creation, Noachian, and Palestinian accounts. Nor does it, at first view, explain the so-called Elohistic and Jehovahistic portions of Genesis. But this is because it has been *assumed* that the name Jehovah was not known before Moses.

It was six hundred years from Abraham to Moses, and during four hundred of those years Israel was in Egypt. That was long enough, under their conditions, to lose the precise theological knowledge which their fathers had received. Hence the use of the Divine name Jehovah fell into disuse in Egypt, and was given again to Moses in Exodus 3 : 13–18 ; 6 : 3. But some think that was the first revelation of it, though in fact it may have been then thus given to distinguish Jehovah from the gods of Egypt. We notice the previous use of Jehovah in Ex. 3 : 2, 4, 7, of events before its revelation in verse 14. (See "God in Creation," p. 61.)

Moreover, it would derogate from the majesty of the record to substitute another word for Jehovah in a passage like, "I have waited for Thy salvation, O Jehovah !" (Gen. 49 : 18.) So of Joseph, it is not simply a God who was with him in Egypt, but JEHOVAH (39 : 2), which is repeated in verses 3, 5, 21, 23. Properly to his master's wife, Joseph urges that it was sin against God—against her God as well as his God, and so Jehovah is not used, but the general name for God (verse 9). In 28 : 13, 16, 21 Jehovah again appears as the Covenant Lord of Israel, whom Leah recognized in 29 : 31, 32, 35. Nor was the word used without a purpose by Isaac in Gen. 26 : 2, 12, 22, 24, 25, 28, 29, seven times in that chapter. And it seems to be of special significance as used in chapters 22, 19, 18, 17, 16, 15, and 14 : 22, being the name of the Covenanted Jehovah, where the God of Melchizedek is distinguished from the Jehovah of Abraham. He does not cast off Hagar, but His angel found her at the fountain, and bade her return to her mistress (16 : 7, 9, 11, 13). It is hardly probable that Moses made such changes in the text, though he might properly revise local names and add a word of illustration. Thus in 14 : 7, 8, 14, where he describes the country as that of the Amalekites, and what was Zoar and Dan ; perhaps inserting verse 19 in chapter 15, and defining Beer-sheba in 26 : 33. In 35 : 20 he observes that Rachel's pillar still remained over her grave, and he makes additions and revisions to chapter 36 : 11, 12, 15, 16, 42, 43. But we prefer to regard the general record as that which was first written, though the modernizing of local names improves the narrative.

Even if we must allow the change of the Divine name by Moses as editor, that is little in comparison with assuming the whole of Genesis to have been a new revelation to Moses, which does not accord with God's usual method of not repeating Himself. And we avoid such repetitions by ascribing the first Genesis to Abraham and his immediate successors. After Moses, not till Samuel, perhaps not till Ezra, was another revision necessary for Hebrew or for Gentile. To Abraham God is revealed as the covenant God; to Moses the ritual of His worship is revealed.

Thus we find sufficient explanation of the differences in style, of local names, of words free and flowing, or concise and rigid, of the scientific, prophetic, narrative, and poetic writing of our Genesis.

Dr. Cave properly asks, " If Moses was the Jehovist, who was the Elohist ?" And then gives reasons for believing that he was both. " He utilized existing materials collected by a writer who preferred the name Elohim for Deity, and he, there is strong reason for believing, was the Jehovistic writer ; for he might well have penned his Elohistic document a sufficient time before the events at Sinai to account for the change of literary style, as well as of religious standpoint." Yes, Dr. Cave, he might; but did he ? And does this explain what St. Stephen said about him, and what he supposed his brethren understood of him? Dr. Cave seems not to account for St. Stephen, in his able defence of the Mosaic authorship. But we must account for that, and for Moses's first mistake and failure. These are points which strongly make for Abraham as the original writer of the first portions of our Genesis, while Isaac, Jacob, and Judah wrote the succeeding chapters.

§ X.—*Abraham's Memoirs.*

The patriarch, having revised and corrected what he had been early taught, and incorporated what had been revealed to him of the Creation Story and the primitive history of mankind in chapters 1 to 11, proceeds, in chapter 12, to record his personal memoirs. Who but Abraham could write Genesis 12? It contains the call to him to get out of his country, from his kindred, and from his father's house, unto a land which God would show him, and there make of him a great nation. This is a personal communication which he regarded as from Jehovah. It took him up by the roots, so to say, cut through his affections, and implied manifold risks in following. He was comparatively a young man of some sixty years when he left Ur. He spent some more years in Haran, where his father died, and in his seventy-fifth year was bidden to pass on to Shechem and the oak of Moreh. These are all matters known only to Abraham at the first. But they were so vitally important to him that he could not let them float away into uncertain memories, and so he duly entered the account in his register.

But because he added, to emphasize the peculiar fact of God's gift of the land to him and his posterity, "And the Canaanite was then in the land," some hold that another wrote it at a later time. It is, in fact, a time-mark of antiquity. It was not written in Egypt, nor at Sinai, nor under conquering Joshua, but by him to whom the country was promised when the Canaanite was in the land. Abraham evidently considered it a proof of God's purpose to put him in their place.

Others have kept a diary of events, even writing down impressive dreams. Here is the root and foundation of a new and Revealed Religion, by which the God of heaven entered into covenant with man; a representative man, religious, intelligent, prosperous, and with a remarkable opportunity opening before him—think you that such a man, having the ability to write, would fail to record and carefully preserve such a Divine promise to him and to his seed? Promptly he builded an altar unto the LORD, and upon going to Bethel he built another (verses 7, 8). As the greater would seem to include the less, we infer that he also wrote the account of all these matters for the use of his promised seed, through whom all families of men should be blessed (verse 3). He also records his visit to Egypt, because of the famine in Canaan; what befell him there, and his safe return, being very rich in cattle, in silver and in gold. It was twenty years before the birth of Isaac. Lot also was with him (12 : 10 ; 13 : 1).

Surely these things were not matters of a later revelation. And representations of similar visits are to-day found upon Egyptian monuments. Syrian nomads are portrayed as entering the Delta and obtaining permission to pasture their flocks and herds. Even on the tomb of an Egyptian governor of the era of Abraham is represented a company of Syrians coming to him for permission to pasture their herds in his district. The reigning Pharaoh was probably Usertesen II., of the twelfth dynasty. One of the best-known pictures of the ancient empire represents the arrival of a nomad chief, with his family and dependents, seeking sustenance and protection. They were Semites from Arabia, or Palestine. Even the name of the chief is given, Abshah, which some identify with that of Abraham. It at least suggests that where Abshah was received Abraham would not be rejected.

Moreover, presents like those of the Pharaoh to Abraham—viz., sheep, oxen, asses, and slaves, are to-day found pictured on the monuments of Beni-Hassan. They mark an early period, since after the ass became the emblem of Typho he would not be thus represented ; nor would they whose god he symbolized give him away to unbelievers ; nor would true Egyptians present to their friends what they regarded as emblems of the Devil ; for such in later times the ass became in Egypt. This portraiture, then, belongs to the time before the Hyksos and before the horse was domesticated in the Nile land. It was probably not known there in Abraham's day. Yet the wagons and chariots mentioned in Gen. 45, 46, 50, where horsemen also occur, show that then horses were in common use in Egypt. There is an account in one of the oldest existing papyri of an Egyptian by the name of Saneha, who went as a fugitive to southern Palestine, as a modern would go to a country of which he was suspicious of his safety, and was not quite sure of returning. At length he was restored to his friends, and gave the narrative of his courteous reception and entertainment, and was himself pleased with his welcome home again. ("Records of the Past," vol. vi., pp. 131-150; also vol. ii. of 2d ed., with a new translation by M. Maspero).

Of chapter 13 there can be no question that Abraham, rather than Lot, was the writer. Its contents would not be a revelation to Moses. It is history. So of the memorable incidents in Gen. 14; they were evidently recorded by its chief actor. The supposed difficulty in verse 7, "They smote all the country of the Amalekites," disappears if considered as the revision of Moses. Amalek is here first mentioned, but not by anticipation, as the "Speaker's Commentary" suggests, nor as a powerful people of uncertain origin, so the "Concise Dictionary of Religious Knowledge," but as a later revision which described the smitten country as that which was occupied by the Amalekites. It was the field or country where they dwelt in the time of Moses or the reviser. They were descended from Esau (Gen. 36 : 16).

Chapter 14 also shows the mistake of Lot. He had made his choice, and dwelt in the cities of the Plain, when Chedorlaomer appeared and captured him with all he possessed. The details are so explicit respecting names and nations in Syria and South Babylonia, the number of Abraham's trained servants and his allies, the way taken to Hobah, and the rescue by a night attack of all the persons and property that had been carried away; the happy return, the public thanksgiving by the priest-king of Salem, the bread and wine brought forth, the tithes paid by Abraham, even the little strategy of the prince of Sodom in order to gain some honor for himself among his subjects, after his defeat by the marauders, and the refusal of Abraham to take any share of the recovered goods for his risk and pains, save only what the young soldiers had eaten, the portion due to Aner, Eschol, and Mamre— these are so many marks of time and circumstance as to require a prompt record of the particulars to be made by the chief actor in the occurrences. They were not the things to be left to inspiration in some later writer, but were written out and handed on from Abraham to Moses, or the fine distinction between the El-Elyon of Melchizedek and the Jehovah El-Elyon of Abraham loses all its point (14 : 22). Pentateuchal analysts overlook its importance. See an able paper by Rev. H. A. Rogers in O. and N. Test. Student for March, 1890.

The vision and revelation narrated in chapter 15 ; the promise of an heir other than Ishmael, notwithstanding the prayer of his father ; the gift of all the country round about the Jordan ; the accompanying sacrifice and the attesting fire, together with the dark unfolding of the servitude of his descendants for four hundred years, to be followed by judgments upon the oppressors and the deliverance of Israel, with the boundaries of the lands they should possess—these, too, were recorded by Abraham. They were of such far-seeing importance as not to be left to the chance of memory and erring traditions.

That it was early attributed to Moses finds illustration in our English translation of the Bible, which is often attributed to Coverdale, or Rogers, or Cranmer, or even to Wycliffe, or to Geneva, instead of to William Tyndale, to whom the first half of the Old Testament and the whole of the New Testament should be ascribed, with revisions by Coverdale, Rogers, and later editors.

In Gen. 16 are family incidents and details of a character which none but the parties directly concerned could preserve ; which Abraham could write only in part, and which found a completing hand in Judah. For it would be strange indeed if he did not cross the track of Hagar's grandchildren. Those shepherds and hunters were not strangers to one another. The man who knew the children of Midian also knew the children of Ishmael (37 : 26-28). Thus he was competent to add to the tribal history, by gleanings from others of Abraham's family. Attentive readers of the Bible are often pained at the notions of those who claim to find in its narrative portions the same measure of inspiration as they find in its visions, its Divine Epiphanies, and its covenant revelations.

The angel's announcement to Hagar in regard to her son, the sort of man he would be, and the position he would occupy are not beneath the dignity of history. It was not, however, a revelation to Moses. If no other use comes of knowing about Ishmael, it at least teaches the difference in those who were in the line of redemptive preparations and those who were not. And it discloses the human factors engaged therein : how human impulse, if not passion, conduced to the one great end ; how the pride of Sarah, in discarding Ishmael, prepared a place for the Babe of Bethlehem. Indeed, the free play (we use the word reverently) of the human with the Divine marks the truth of the story in Genesis, as well as the Scribe who penned it for after ages. But they would not be revelations given four centuries later.

Chapter 17 to 18 : 15 narrates the institution of circumcision as the seal of Jehovah's covenant with

His chosen people ; how Canaan was bestowed upon them as an everlasting possession ; how Israel was promised as the heir of that covenant ; how Abraham was circumcised in his ninety-ninth year, and Ishmael in his thirteenth year, as well as all the men born in his house, or bought with money— free-born and slave-born were circumcised with their tribal chief. They are personal items of wide-reaching significance, and so were faithfully recorded at the time. It was, in fact, the *Magna Charta* of Jehovah renewed to Abraham and to the posterity of Sarah : in Isaac was the chosen race. Thus early was Woman's Rights certified by Covenant. Not in Ishmael, not in after-born sons of Keturah, but in the gentle Isaac, the child of Abraham in his hundredth year and of Sarah in her ninetieth year, was the covenant to be sealed and the nations to be blessed. Can we doubt that records of that Divine heritage were made at the time, and by him whom God called out of Ur to become its chief human agent? It is not to be expected that supernal means would be used to perpetuate or to give new accounts of what could just as well be written and transcribed by human hands and a truthful spirit.

Thus was penned the visit of the angels whom Abraham entertained, and who made known to him coming events, and what God was about to do to the wicked cities of southern Jordan. That memorable appeal to the Divine clemency, which has rendered the patriarch forever illustrious as the great interceder for great sinners, was written soon after it was made. Simple in its grandeur, it sets forth the progressive steps in the plea to save the obdurate: "If fifty, if lack of five of fifty, if forty, and so on down to ten"—who but Abraham could have pleaded so earnestly and so adroitly at that time? Who but he could have written it for our learning? Then the LORD went His way after communing with Abraham, and Abraham returned to his place (Gen. 18 : 33). Could such a statement be a revelation to Moses six centuries later? While the incident teaches a striking lesson touching God's dealings with man, it has little special relation with Israel, or with later unfoldings to him. But the judgment removed one set of corrupt people from contamination of others. No parallel has yet been discovered to that famous pleading.

§ XI.—*Destruction of Sodom in Accadian Legend.*

But of the dire calamity which followed, even of the deliverance of Lot, though not of his prayer, all which are related in Gen. 19, an account is believed to have been found in the Babylonian inscriptions. We read thus: "An overthrow from the midst of the deep there came. The fated punishment from the midst of heaven descended. A storm like a plummet the earth overwhelmed. To the four winds the destroying flood like fire did burst. The inhabitants of cities it caused to be tormented; their bodies it consumed. In city and country it spread death, and the flames as they rose overthrew. Freemen and slaves were equal, and the high places it filled. In heaven and earth it rained a thunderstorm. Death overtook mankind. As for this man [probably Lot] there was a loud voice of the thunder [to warn him]. The terrible lightning flash descended. During the day it flashed; grievously it fell." ("Records of the Past," vol. xi., pp. 117-18.) However that inscription was derived, the account originated with Abraham as recorded in our Genesis. The name Lot is supposed to be found in Syrian inscriptions.

The avenging downpour of fire from heaven, burning and consuming the earth, destroyed a land which had been as the garden of Eden. It is a catastrophe which finds confirmation in the history of the allied chieftains under Chedorlaomer. They were heads of tribes and principalities in southern Babylonia. Nimrod is believed to have had a successor in one of them, and all of them in their successors were merged and consolidated by Sargon of Agâde, the list of whose names and reigns was found and displayed by Naram-Sin, the son of Sargon, when hard pushed by his unassimilated subjects. This list, thus composed and originating, probably formed the long line of 350 kings whom Naram-Sin claimed to have reigned before him; and it has needlessly revolutionized the old Babylonian chronology. Some critics seem ready to accept any pretence for putting dates and eras back as far as possible, as though such change could affect the truth of history. Not only was there a beginning to historic times, but such beginning bore some relation to other and contemporaneous events. Sargon I. and his son prove and illustrate the unification of four or five different lines of princes, who were, in fact, contemporaneous.

Indeed, the confederacy and expedition of Chedorlaomer against southern Palestine, render the legend of the Accadians concerning it, not only not surprising, but, under the circumstances, quite natural. For the survivors could report, after their defeat by Abraham, that those who had rebelled against their authority "were destroyed by Anu, who rained fire upon them from heaven in punishment for their rebellion." And so great was the importance attached to the account of it, that it is found in "the original Accadian text of the tablet as well as in the Assyrian translation of it" (Professor Sayce). This fragment of a very ancient tablet, which has been preserved to our day, confirms Abraham's account of the Overthrow of Sodom and Gomorrah. It was translated in 1878, from the "Cuneiform Inscriptions of Western Asia."

There are eighteen lines of Accadian and Assyrian text, written a thousand miles distant from the place of destruction, which disclose a contemporary record of that catastrophe.

But the ten verses which follow the account in

Gen. 19 are to be ascribed to Moses, who enacted the infliction of a penalty for the sin there related, and in Deut. 23 : 3 forbade the descendants of Lot to enter the assembly of the LORD to the tenth generation.

Properly enough such a character as Lot drops out of the patriarch's memoirs. It would seem that uncle and nephew never again met. Moses may have obtained the record of Ammon and Moab through the family of Judah or of Jethro. He certainly encountered them while on the way to Palestine, when they sent for Balaam to curse Israel. It was a poor return for Lot's being twice saved by Abraham's interposition ; but the ingratitude of their father reappeared in his descendants. (See Num. 22, 23, 24.)

§ XII.—*Some Domestic Events.*

The episode of the patriarch with Abimelech of Gerar in Gen. 20, which, like a two-edged sword, cuts both, was not derived from the Philistines. Nor was it the sort of matter to be revealed to Moses ; and it bears every mark of the record of a prime actor in it. Its ethical lesson is similar to that of chapter 12, and was early incorporated by Abraham into his family history.

In chapter 21 we have the Divine announcement of Isaac's birth, of his circumcision when eight days old, his father being then a hundred years old, and that Sarah laughed for joy of having Isaac, whose name means, "he laughs;" also the account of her wounded pride that the son of Hagar was mocking, perhaps quite playfully, at the pranks of the boy when Isaac was weaned. These are things which Abraham was the fittest person living to enter in the family register. They are not the matters for special revelation. So of the weaning of Isaac and the feast which celebrated that event, the father, or his scribe, would record it. Of Sarah's increasing jealousy of Hagar and Ishmael, whom her pride could no longer tolerate near her; of their expulsion from among her thousand domestics; of God's word to Abraham touching the lad and his mother, and how his strong parental love clave to his firstborn, of whom Heaven promised to make a nation; of Abraham's early rising in the morning, preparing the outfit of bread and a bottle-skin of water, perhaps also adding some silver current at that time, and then sending mother and boy away—these are just the things which Abraham would write down, so that in the future of his two sons each would know that their father had dealt kindly by them. This was attested later on by Ishmael as well as Isaac attending the burial of the patriarch. Nor was there any after strife between those sons.

But the account of the wanderings of the lad and his mother in the wilderness of Beersheba; of his weariness and fainting; of her hearing the angel, who came to answer the voice of the lad whom God had heard; of her seeing the water-well and refilling her bottle-skin for Ishmael; of his reviving and growing to be an archer, and that Hagar took a wife for him out of her own native Egypt—all this *extra* covenant history was probably collected by Judah, or obtained from Jethro, and incorporated by Moses.

With 21 : 22 is resumed the register of Abraham. The interview of Abimelech and Phichol, which ended in a treaty and a present to seal it with those Philistine chiefs, all joining in a covenant at Beersheba; the tree-planting, the calling upon "Jehovah, the Everlasting God, and Abraham's sojourn in the Philistines' land many days," are related by the patriarch. It is family history written at the time, and not a new revelation to another, nor later obtained from the Philistines.

The first nineteen verses of chapter 22, touching the offering of Isaac, form one of the most striking episodes in the patriarch's life. It tries his faith in God, proves his character, tests his manhood, and illustrates the Divine wisdom in the choice of such a man to be the founder of a new nation for the Light of the world. For Messianic preparation and the instruction of the nations in religion, it had a wide-reaching significance. And it was Heaven's prohibition of human sacrifice. Abraham was tempted to sacrifice Isaac, and then forbidden to do it, a substitute being provided in a ram for a burnt offering. The Divine manifesto was spread abroad. (See "Bible Growth and Religion," pp.

58, 80, 81.) Every line of the record was written by Abraham, and every sentence of it was graven on his heart. Criticism is dumb before it. Analysis of it becomes reverent admiration. It also portrays the history of the chosen race, when condemned and scattered to the four winds; and as Isaac was restored to his father, so shall Israel be restored to the favor of their covenant God.

The last five verses are a part of the family records as kept by his brother Nahor in Haran, and introduce the genealogy of Rebekah, who became Isaac's wife. Hence their importance in the history of Israel. It is a reproach upon Hebrew strictness in such matters to suppose that such details would be neglected.

And now another trial befell the patriarch. At the age of one hundred and twenty-seven years, Sarah, the proud mother of Isaac, died. The account is in Gen. 23, and the particulars of the purchase of the field of Machpelah from the sons of Heth. The treaty then made; the stipulated price of 400 shekels of silver passing with the merchants of the time, being rather more than $200, but worth many times that amount now; the procession to the gate of the city to acknowledge the transaction, like men before a notary public, or town clerk, to register the transfer of real estate to-day; all was done to ratify the purchase by Abraham of that field and the cave in it, for a burying place, of the sons of Heth (23 : 20).

The words, "the same is Hebron," v. 2, was a later addition.

The care here manifested to make sure the transfer of the property thus publicly bought, was reason enough for the purchaser to enter the facts upon the papyrus, or prepared skins used for writing his memoirs.

It was a princess who had died after a happy marriage of nearly a century. The burial was with due honor and circumstance. Abraham and Isaac were there, and the mourners of an immense household—at least twelve hundred. It was a most impressive event in that family history. Here also, in after years, Abraham, Isaac, and Jacob were severally laid to rest, in presence of a mourning assembly, and none ever disputed their title to the land. That is strong evidence of a treaty and deed of transfer. And the evidence presented by recent decipherments of the habit of writing in Babylonia, whence Abraham came, in Palestine, where he long dwelt, and in Egypt, which he visited, would reduce him to an insignificant man, if he did not record the important events of his long career. The friend of God was not a dunce among men.

Inscriptions show that some of those Hittites could wage successful war and make enduring treaties. It was about the time when Accadian literature was in full bloom ; a century after Amenemhat I. wrote his "Instructions" to his son, probably the earliest literary production of a royal pen that has come down to us; it was not far from the story of Sancha's flight from Thebes to Palestine, when writing was well known ("Ancient Empires of the East," p. 29; "Bible Growth and Religion," pp. 75, 136-39.)

In Gen. 24 we have confirmation of this writing habit in the records concerning the sworn agreement between Abraham and his chief servant touching the procuring of a wife for Isaac. With the utmost solemnity the elder was enjoined to visit Abraham's kindred in Haran, and there select the destined bride. The domestic scene is so minutely portrayed: the daughters of the land tending and watering their flocks; the recorded prayer of the servant; the damsel's courtesy to him and her brother's hospitality; the announcement of the purpose of his visit, attested by the costly presents he had brought and placed on Rebekah (verse 22); his cordial reception and welcome by Laban; the speedy delivery of his message from Abraham, with an account of his prosperity, and that he had a son who must not come to Haran, but a bride be taken to him from thence—all which is repeated with verbal exactness; compare verses 4-9 with 34-41; also compare 12-24 with 42-48. The servant's prayer-test was answered. He could but ask that Rebekah should go with him to Isaac. He was in haste, but was not precipitate with his errand, feeling sure of success. And the consent of the family and of the damsel followed. Then other presents were given, vessels of silver, and jewels of gold, and raiment for Rebekah, with precious things for her mother and brother. Properly it was left for the damsel to decide whether she wished longer time for preparation, or would go at once to her new home. "I will go," she said. Never was a more speedy betrothal and never a happier marriage. For they all knew the character of Abraham and were assured about his son. So away sped Rebekah to Isaac. He was found in prayerful meditation in his field at the eventide. And Isaac took Rebekah, and she became his wife.

Here are sixty-seven verses of one of the longest chapters in Genesis narrating scenes in domestic life whose importance to Israel and the world centres in the fact that they account for the family origin of the chosen people. They are descended in blood relation from the same Semitic tribe. It is in Isaac and Rebekah, from the same ancestry, that the promise of Man's Redemption was sealed. In this grand fact alone centres our interest in that bridal meeting. The dismounting of the bride, the veiling of herself when Isaac approached, the report of the servant, and the noted omission of a feast, out of respect for the memory of Sarah—all this marks the account as made at the time. It is clearly narrative rather than the revelation of a later age. And the report of the servant, and the prayer he offered, and the answer of Rebekah, were incorporated into the family history soon after their safe arrival in the home of Abraham. They were matters of too much importance to be relegated to strangers, and yet they were not matters of revelation, but facts to be recorded. An account written some centuries later would contain some errors : a marriage-feast would be inserted, and the present order of those sixty-seven verses of Gen. 24 would be changed. But as they now stand, with the part of the several actors at Haran and the later home-making, without a shade of color derived from Jacob's experiences with Laban in after days, we have Abraham, the chief servant, Rebekah and Isaac, all parties concerned in a true account, and attesting to this part of the family records of the covenant-race. With chapter 24 the personal memoirs of Abraham end, and Isaac continues the narrative.

§ XIII.—*Isaac's Memoirs.*

These commence, we may assume, with Gen. 25 : 1. Possibly verses 5 and 6 are by Abraham, but the account of Ishmael and his sons was given by Judah (verses 12–19). The "gifts" to Keturah's sons recall the gifts to Hagar ; compare 21 : 14 with 25 : 6. They included enough of silver and herds to enable the sons to make a fair start in life. The half-brothers never troubled Isaac about a more generous share of their father's property. This would imply a fair apportionment upon the separation. The patriarch was a rich man when he left Egypt. "He had sheep, and oxen, and asses, and camels, men servants and women servants; was very rich in cattle, in silver, and in gold" (Gen. 12 : 16; 13 : 2). His trained servants, born in his household, numbered 318 when he pursued and routed Chedorlaomer with his allies. He lived prosperously after that time for about ninety-five years. So he must have left a large estate, which in these days of courts and surrogates would feed lawsuits for a generation. But the fair dealing of Abraham was so marked that no disturbance arose because of Isaac having more than Ishmael, or Midian, or Shuah. It suggests intelligence as well as nobility of character, which provided an equitable division of his property. His learning was more than that of a prosperous shepherd and chief of a tribe of nomads, and he had various accomplishments.

If he was the original of "Father Orham" in Ur, and the peer of any in that place, or in Haran, when he left it; if he was treated as a prince in Egypt by the Pharaohs of the twelfth dynasty; if the kings of Canaan so treated him, and were wholly indebted to him for successful generalship in the defeat of Babylonian oppressors; if the Priest-king of Salem and the King of Sodom blessed and honored him; if Abimelech of Gerar sought his alliance and made a treaty with him; if he was able to converse in their different languages with the peoples whom he met in Haran, in Canaan, and in Egypt; if, above and beyond all this, he was favored with hearing Divine voices, seeing Divine visions, and receiving Divine communications, which have been carefully preserved to this day, then it is but just to his memory to allow him sufficient skill to keep his own record of those things in which he was a most important actor, and so deeply concerned. Among other legacies he committed those records to his son Isaac as containing matters worthy of preservation.

Moreover, at his death, Jacob and Esau were some fifteen years old, and able to remember much of what their grandfather had told them. Chapters 25 to 28 : 9 narrate the additions made by Isaac, and how the blessing of his first-born was given to Jacob : "God Almighty bless thee, and give thee the blessing of Abraham, and to thy seed" (28 : 3, 4).

This abrupt and unexpected change in the order of inheritance in the family, reversing the usual course in those days, implies the existence of a contemporary record. Certainly, any later and uninspired writer would not reverse it ; he would not see the reason for it ; being the facts of history, inspiration would not be required. So this change of the younger for the elder ; the bitter cry of Esau ; the cunning supplanting of Jacob and his consequent flight to Aram, though a puzzle to early readers of that family history, became clear enough to the inspired reviser who wrote for the chosen people in the era of the Exodus. To regard it as a New Revelation to Moses is to interpose a miracle where no miracle is needed.

Moreover, even in the brief section of the family register by Isaac, the supernatural certainly appears. Thus in Gen. 26 : 2-5 and verse 24, two Divine communications to Isaac are recorded. Though pressed by a famine like that which sent Abraham to Egypt, Isaac is told not to go down thither, for the Hyksos were then conquering that land, and the Divine covenant is renewed to him in exclusion of all his half-brothers. He was to seek refuge in Philistine Gerar. After his return and abode at Beersheba, Jehovah again appeared to him, and repeated His blessing upon him and upon his seed. And Isaac builded an altar there, and called upon the name of the Lord (verse 25). The treaty agreement with Abimelech, the feast, the digging of a well, whence it was called "the well of the oath," especially the recorded marriage of Esau to Judith, the daughter of Beeri, the Hittite : "Which were a bitterness of spirit to Isaac and Rebekah," could be written by no one so well as by Isaac. Who else would state the inner, subjective *feeling* of the parents at the marriage of their son—the self-reliant Esau? His going later to Ishmael and taking his daughter Mahalath to wife, though intended to please his parents, was but an attempt to correct the irrevocable ; for he already had two Hittite wives (26 : 34 ; 28 : 9). It was conduct which perhaps no contemporary, except his beloved father, would be likely to record. But with our knowledge of the then prevalent habit of writing, attested by recent decipherments, there can be no objection to saying that Isaac himself wrote down those matters at the time. It was his duty to do so.

Who can read those tender, tearful words of Isaac and Esau (27 : 32-38) without deep sympathy for both father and son, as well as the conviction that they were recorded at the time? It is the affectionate conversation of disappointed parental and filial love. It is desire against destiny. It is the human overruled by Heaven. The reader should study the passage. So assured was Esau of his father's affection for him, that he could not believe it possible that he had no blessing reserved for him before he died! "And he cried with a great and exceeding bitter cry ... Bless me, even me also, O my father! ... Hast thou not reserved a blessing for me? Hast thou but one blessing, my father? bless me, even me also, O my father. And Esau lifted up his voice, and wept." Then his father gave him the blessing of earth, its fatness, and the dew of heaven, but not the blessing of Jehovah; and he should serve his brother (verses 39, 40). There is nothing superior to it in love and pathos in Hebrew literature. Not a later revelation to Moses, it was the recorded words of Isaac and Esau, and was written by the father in the family history.

This view is emphasized by what is said of the hate of Esau for Jacob, and his purposed revenge for loss of the Divine blessing. It was told to Rebekah, who told it to Jacob, and hastened his flight to her kindred in Haran. "Tarry there till thy brother's anger turn away from thee, and he forget what thou hast done to him" (verses 41-45); for he was known to be of a generous disposition. Rebekah's words to Isaac in verse 46, containing her reasons for sending Jacob to her brother Laban, with Isaac's charge to Jacob about taking a wife from his own kindred, and then giving him the blessing of God Almighty, and the blessing of Abraham, to him and his seed, which blessing God gave to Abraham (28 : 1-5), also belong to the register of Isaac, as well as the account of Esau in verses 6-9. Here end the memoirs of Isaac; to which may be added the account of his death (35 : 27-29). But chapter 36 was by Judah, revised by Moses, giving the family register of Esau and his descendants. Perhaps verse 31 was by a writer as late as Samuel, who added that the list of "the Kings there given of Edom was before there reigned any king over Israel." Thus, all seeming difficulties in Genesis are cleared up, if we accept the now apparent *fact* of a Divine revelation written out by the patriarchs, and later adapted by the prophets to the needs of their age.

Only to distinguish the other branches of Abraham's descendants from the Israelites is the record admitted into Genesis, and also to show that Job and his friends were of their kindred, though not of the covenant seed (36 : 10, 15, 28 ; 25 : 2) ; Job was of Uz and an Esauite.

To suppose that a writing people, such as we know the Hebrews then were, did not record important events in their family history, is absurd. Indeed, such exercises probably occupied much of their leisure. Those blessings of Isaac are unique. His carefulness in using the Divine name marks him as a man accustomed to think. No late writer would so discriminate. Esau should become great, but not with the spiritual unfoldings and blessings of Jacob. Nay, he should serve his brother, till he broke his yoke from off him (27 : 38-40). Compare 36 : 6-8, " And Esau took his wives, and his sons, and his daughters, and all his household, his cattle, his beasts, and all his substance, and went into the country of Mount Seir, from the face of his brother Jacob." Their riches and pursuits required a larger land than Canaan, in which they were but sojourners ; and Esau remembered that the inheritance of the home estate belonged to Jacob, by his own agreement and his father's will. These are so many indications of an early record, and also account for differences in style and language. They disclose the several authors of Genesis. The early patriarchs were skilled in writing, and taught it to their sons. According to Eupolemus, Abraham resided during his stay in Egypt in the sacred city of On or Heliopolis, and at that seat of learning and religion he taught the Egyptians astronomy and arithmetic. So Rawlinson.

§ XIV. — *The Memoirs of Jacob.*

These evidently begin at Gen. 28 : 10, "And Jacob left Beersheba, and went toward Haran." Then he gives the events of his journey, his wonderful dream of the angels passing up and down the ladder, and the appearance of the LORD standing above it, and identifying Himself to him as the LORD, the God of Abraham and of Isaac. Then the promise: "The land whereon thou liest, to thee will I give it, and to thy seed. It shall greatly increase and spread abroad, and be a blessing to all families of men." Notice verse 15, "And, behold, I am with thee, and will keep thee whithersoever thou goest, and will bring thee again into this land; for I will not leave thee, until I have done that which I have spoken to thee of." As well ask a bride to forget her husband as to suppose that Jacob did not record that Divine promise. It made such an impression upon him that he awoke out of his sleep, and said, "Surely the LORD is in this place; and I knew it not." That abode of God and gate of heaven filled him with fear and reverence. He rose early in the morning, and set up a pillar-stone of witness, pouring oil upon it, and vowed unto God, according to the tenor of the dream, that if God would be with him, and keep him in the way he went, and give him bread to eat, and raiment to put on, so that he returned to his father's house in peace, then, he says, "Shall the LORD be my God, and this stone, set up for a pillar, shall be God's house : and of all that Thou givest me I will surely give a tenth unto Thee" (verses 16-22). Such important details were not long left to memory, and the change of name from Luz to Beth-el emphasized the importance of the vision and covenant. It explained that not in Ishmael, not in Esau, but in Jacob was the line of descent of the people of Jehovah.

Abraham was given to understand it in his hundredth year ; Isaac was given to understand it in his twofold blessing of his sons ; and now Jacob, who had been rather sharp, through his mother's instigation, in dealing with Esau, is enabled to understand that it was not by any act of his own, though accepted by his brother, but by this promise and renewal of covenant by God Himself with him, that he is appointed the head of his tribe and the blessed of Heaven. It was a transaction which concerned him and his descendants, and which he carefully wrote out for them. They were not matters for later revelation, nor to be gathered from varying traditions, but were duly entered in the family register by its newly appointed chief. While in Laban's service, Jacob had opportunity for literary exercises, and the skill he displayed in after times, upon his return home, while dwelling in Shechem, and when he stood before Pharaoh and "blessed him," indicating his feeling of equality with, if not his superiority over the Egyptian king

—all this indicates capacity and mental training which easily includes the ability to write.

Who but Jacob could write Gen. 28 : 10-22 ? Who but the lover of Rachel, who kissed her at the well, and would not be content with her sister Leah, could write chapter 29 : 1-35, making Judah the son of Leah, but not of Rachel the beloved ? Surely if internal evidence has any weight in this matter, it carries the proof of contemporaneous authorship on the face of the record. Our text makes the two most prominent names and characters in the after history of Israel to be the sons of the less loved Leah. Levi and Judah were her sons. It is evidence of a Divine purpose overruling human choice and affection ; a purpose seen in the appointment of Isaac instead of Ishmael, of Jacob instead of Esau, and of the sons of Leah instead of Rachel's beloved boys. Such *unexpectedness* marks alike the origin and the inspiration of the account. For nothing but God's guidance of later copyists of these records would allow it to stand as we find it. The best days of Israel were marked by reverence for her priests, and her golden age was full of the praises of David, yet her ancient writings recorded that Judah and Levi were the sons of the less loved but first wife of Jacob. So, in the face of all learned criticism of these annals, it is safe to affirm that no later writer, when the priests were powerful and David was king, would have failed to represent Levi and Judah as the sons of the best loved Rachel. That the text makes them the sons of Leah stamps its origin. That, amid all the changes in dynasty and ritual after Solomon, the text remained and remains to our day, making Levi and Judah Leah's sons, seals alike its inspired truthfulness and its Divine preservation. Jacob first wrote it in his family register.

The entire contents of chapter 30 are also by Jacob. In 31 : 1, 2, we find additional proof: "Jacob heard the words of Laban's sons, saying, he hath taken away all that was our father's. . . . And Jacob beheld the countenance of Laban . . . it was not toward him as formerly." These are the observations of a contemporary recorder of what he saw and heard. But verse 3 is a Divine revelation: "The LORD said unto Jacob, Return unto the land of thy fathers, and to thy kindred; and I will be with thee." He proceeds at once to arrange for his return; he had a joint interview with Rachel and Leah, and recounted his grievances; he also told them of God's appearances to him at Beth-el and more recently. And Rachel and Leah—the order of names marks the record as Jacob's, placing the best loved first—answered, Is there any portion or inheritance for us in our father's house? Are we not counted of him strangers? There was nothing in the after-history of Laban's immediate descendants which provoked the hostility of Israel, and so only its truth could have induced a contemporary writer to detail these particulars so disparaging to Laban. So also were the blending of the human with the Divine in the flight of Jacob and the pursuit after him (verses 22-30). with loss of his gods—probably images of the Moon-god, who was worshipped in Haran (verses 30-35).

Jacob's indignation at Laban's charging him with stealing his gods, or the teraphim with which he worshipped, could not have been invented by any late historian of Israel. Under Judges like Gideon and Jephthah such conduct would cause no surprise. In the account of Micah, the Ephraimite, and of the Danites, who despoiled him at once of priest and ephod, images and teraphim, we find an aggravated parallel. While after Solomon, who built chapels for the use of his foreign wives in the worship of their gods, no writer would invent the just indignation of Jacob, who had so recently heard God speaking to him. The passage is, therefore, a time-mark of ancient authorship, and suggests that the accused Jacob was its writer. Compare Gen. 31 : 22-42 ; Jud. 8 : 24-28 ; 11 : 1-40 ; 17 ; 18 ; 1 Kings 11 : 1-10.

So Gen. 31 : 43-55, stating Laban's *claim* as the father of his daughters to their children, and to all that Jacob had with them, even his cattle, and all born unto him, would appear absurd to a Hebrew after Moses, whose legislation made each father the head of his family, his wife being adopted into the family of her husband. I indeed marvel that men of learning should overlook such time-marks of authorship. None but Jacob could have penned the account of the treaty-making, where " no man was witness" (verse 50); but God was witness, the pillar-heap was witness, and their mutual oath was witness. While the invocation of the God of Abraham, and the God of Nahor, as their God, was proper for the time, yet that Jacob should " swear by the Fear of his father Isaac," and then " offer sacrifice upon the mount" is unique and original, of high antiquity, and not according to the law of Moses (verses 53, 54). The good-by in verse 55 is the record of Jacob.

Moreover, Jacob alone could write chapter 32. The vision of angels at Mahanaim, the name he gave to the place where he saw the hosts of heaven in readiness to help him; his message to Esau, the exact number and names of the presents to him, also the number of his brother's escort, with the feelings the news caused in Jacob; his dividing his flocks and belongings into two bands, so that if smitten, one party might escape, suggest the prudence of the maker of the second bargain with Laban, and of the vow at Beth-el. Even his prayer to the God of his fathers is characteristic; it is part biographical, part reminiscent, and part petition (32 : 9-12). No one but Jacob could write that prayer. He also wrote verses 13-23. So of that memorable vision at Peniel (verses 24-30), whose name means " the face of God," where alone with a Divine Person Jacob wrestled during that anxious night and obtained his desire, when he was left with a blessing and a mark—who but the wrestler himself could write it? Whether in vision or in essence, Jacob believed that he there saw God, and though his life was preserved, yet he ever afterward bore about the Divine mark (verse 31). But verse 32 was by a later copyist and reviser. Chapters 33 and 34 were by Jacob, who had personal knowledge of all therein related. The return to Beth-el in chapter 35, and the building of an altar there, another appearance of God to him, proving Himself by recalling His former appearance when Jacob fled from his brother, and again blessing him, and changing his name to Israel, and the promise to give that land to him and to his seed after him, and the consecrated pillar set up in memorial of it—this was the record of Jacob of those striking incidents at Luz, which he called El-beth-el, because God there appeared to him (35 : 7).

There, too, Rebekah's nurse, Deborah, died (verse 8), she who had watched over him from infancy, and she was buried at the oak of weeping in Beth-el. Who but this chief among his contemporaries would so honor his old nurse at Beth-el, and enroll her name in the register of his family? Later in the history she would have been buried without the city walls, without the town limits, but this ancient record makes her remains interred beneath, or close to the oak of the sanctuary. It proves the origin and antiquity of these memoirs.

Then, while on the way from Beth-el to Ephrath, beloved Rachel, with the birth of Benjamin, the son of his right hand, died, and was buried. And Jacob set a pillar upon her grave; and there it remained when a later writer copied the record of Jacob (verse 20). The rest of the chapter was also by Jacob, who had not then learned to write his name Israel, reverently shrinking from using the Divine name in it (viz., El, verse 22, last sentence, and verse 29). But verse 21 and first four fifths of 22 may have been by a later hand. Significant is the statement in verse 29, And Isaac gave up the ghost, and died, being old and full of days. And his sons Esau and Jacob buried him. The placing of Esau before Jacob shows the writing to be Jacob's. No later writer would have done it; and with it the Memoirs of Jacob merge into those of Judah.

§ XV.—*Memoirs of Judah.*

On page 79 I have assigned chapter 36, except verse 31, to Judah; verse 31 may have been added by Samuel, who studied and copied the Hebrew Scriptures. The chapter itself narrates the genesis of the Edomites as descended from Esau, who was superseded by his brother Jacob, as the heir to the Divine covenant, and the grand figure in it. Perhaps Esau wrote the original sketch, which was filled out and rearranged by Judah, and thus handed down to Moses. It concerns the cousins of Israel through

Esau, and contains nothing opposed to our view of the original writers of Genesis.

But chapter 37 is a different writing. It introduces the matchless story of Joseph and his brethren, thus preparing for the going down to Egypt. It recounts Divine providences and oversight, the feeding of flocks, the dislike of Joseph, and the selling him by his brothers to the Midianites, who were their cousins in descent, and of whose origin we read in chapter 25. Some parts of the story were revelations from God, some were known to one brother, some to another, some to all the twelve and to Jacob. The time of these occurrences may be assigned to the era of the Hyksos, who were making their conquests in Egypt when Isaac was told not to go there, and the writer of them was Judah, the fourth son of Jacob and Leah.

The evidences of reading and writing then are conclusive, and Judah had equal opportunities with any of his brethren. In chapter 37 he figures as the adviser of his brothers, while chapter 38 tells of his signet ring and bracelets. He was probably the recognized Scribe of the tribes, and then about forty years old.

That Judah had a commanding influence over his brothers is seen in 37 : 26, 27 ; and he interposes for them with his father in 43 : 8-10 ; while in 44 : 14, 16, 18-34, he addresses Joseph on their behalf. After Joseph made himself known to his brethren, and sent for his father to come down to

Egypt, then Jacob commissioned Judah to go before, and prepare for him in Goshen; the Septuagint reads "at the city of Heroes, in the land of Rameses (46 : 28 ; 47: 11). Nor is it straining a point in the narrative to say that as it is the records of Judah we are reading, who does not give the name of the agent, the "one" who told Joseph that his father was sick was Judah, and the "one" who told Jacob that Joseph was coming to see him was Judah (48 : 1, 2). So in the grand benediction of the patriarch he said: "Judah, thy brethren shall praise thee: thy hand shall be in the neck of thine enemies; thy father's children shall bow down before thee." Then, very poetically, he compares him to a lion for strength and leadership, and declares by prophetic inspiration, "A sceptre shall not depart from Judah, nor a lawgiver or ruler's staff from between his feet, until he, Shiloh, come, and he shall have the obedience of the peoples." As a sign of royalty, "he shall wash his garments in wine, and his clothing in the blood of grapes." Professor Briggs interprets it, "Judah will assume the leadership of Israel, and lead the nation in its march until they obtain their inheritance" ("Messianic Prophecy," p. 96).

Gen. 49 : 8–12 has been translated in the Revised Version by some twenty-five of the best Hebrew and Greek scholars in England and America, and compared with the Septuagint version made three centuries before any Christian controversy. They agree in assigning the sceptre to Judah until Messiah come, He whose right it is, who has the obedience of the peoples. At Shiloh the tabernacle was set up, and the wanderings of Israel ceased for seven hundred years. But while Judah led the tribes to conquest and the inheritance of their promised lands, he can hardly be said to have held the ruler's staff before David was enthroned as King of Israel. Not till then may royal prerogatives be attributed to him, when he could wash his garments in wine, and his clothes in the blood of grapes, and his teeth be white with milk.

The whole blessing of Jacob has especial reference to the positions of his sons in Canaan; to the regnancy of Judah, the abode of Zebulon and Dan, and the character of Benjamin. After the return from Exile Judah was the representative and governing tribe amid various fortunes down to Herod the Great. To David's son and Lord shall the gathering of the peoples be.

Only some such view of the history and the text is an adequate exposition of what Jacob by the prophetic spirit so grandly uttered. But to make Judah's supremacy begin and end with arrival at the *place* Shiloh is to descend from the heights of heaven to the depths of earth, and to bestow upon him very inconspicuous honor. Whatever the word Shiloh means, the related verses demand an adequate explanation. There surely was no royalty ascribed to Judah at Shiloh. Not till

David and his sons does it find sufficient realization.

The passage Gen. 49 : 57 is evidence that, at that time, Levi had not been set apart as the *priestly* tribe of Israel, which came to pass under Moses. Verse 10 looked beyond Egypt, beyond Shiloh, to where the praises of Jehovah ascended from Zion.

As Judah was present at the death of his father, and attended his burial in the field of Machpelah, he had personal knowledge of all that occurred. He witnessed Joseph's tearful kiss of the departed, and was one of the mourners for seventy days. Probably he was the "messenger" sent by his brethren to Joseph, after the return from Canaan, to arrange respecting their future in Egypt, or proposed departure from it (50 : 15-22). The record also implies that Judah survived Joseph. And it connects itself, so to say, with Ex. 13 : 19 : "Moses took the bones of Joseph with him; for he had straitly sworn the children of Israel, saying, God will surely visit you; and ye shall carry up my bones away hence with you." So Jacob commanded in Gen. 50 : 25.

Thus we find a duly appointed and competent Scribe, who was also the recognized chief of the tribes. How soon Judah's official writing began may be inferred from the narrative. The blow at the loss of Joseph was so severe upon Jacob, that he gave up all interest in life; he rent his clothes, put on sackcloth, and mourned for his son many days. His other sons and daughters vainly tried to comfort him; but he refused, saying, For I will go down into the grave unto my son mourning (37 : 34, 35). Wherefore Judah took up the pen, added chapter 37 to the family history, and, of course, wrote chapter 38. He only could write it. And he learned from his father all the traditions of the chosen race, the interview with Esau, and the later interview with Pharaoh. His genius and capacity, his opportunities and recognized leadership under his father, alike designate Judah as the official Scribe of the Tribes.

Even when his sons brought him the glad tidings that Joseph was yet alive, Jacob's heart almost misgave him whether he could go down to Egypt. He was about one hundred and thirty years old. "And God spake unto Israel in the visions of the night, and said, Jacob, Jacob! And he said, Here am I. And God said, I am the God of thy father: fear not to go down into Egypt; for I will there make of thee a great nation. I will go down with thee into Egypt; and I will surely bring thee up again: and Joseph shall put his hand upon thine eyes" (Gen. 46 : 2–4). For thirteen years hopeless and depressed, this vision comforted and reassured him. He could now leave the land of his fathers and seek a new home with his beloved son in Egypt. He told the Divine communication to his sons, and Judah wrote it in his memoirs. It certainly was not a revelation to Moses; and no uninspired writer would have applied it to Jacob. Ordinary men would have hastened to the long-lost son as soon as informed of his abode and prosperity; that Jacob hesitated marks the antiquity of the incident and Judah's record of it.

Next to Joseph he is the most conspicuous character in that inimitable story, and probably received from his distinguished brother those parts of it in which he himself was not an actor or observer. So, while the several portions may be regarded as a joint contribution to the narrative, it was Judah who arranged and moulded that historic gem which is the delight of the young and the admiration of all ages. As it became known among the Egyptians, it found at least one imitator, whose version has come down to us. (See "Tale of Two Brothers," in Brugsch's "Egypt Under the Pharaohs," vol. i., pp. 309-11; "Records of the Past," vol. vi., pp. 151–56). Of the residence in Egypt we have only glimpses of its commencement and its close, but no history.

Such were the records from which Moses learned the history of his people; and from the Divine promise to Abraham he supposed, according to St. Stephen, that God, by his hand would deliver them. I see no other way of understanding all the facts presented. The records had been written *before* Moses, and he learned the national history and the Divine purpose from them. What else was he doing during the ten years before his hasty action and sudden flight but studying the annals of his race?

He had the *leisure* and the *means to procure a complete copy of all the records of his people.* St. Stephen suggests they were known, and Moses's conduct implies the same. He certainly was familiar with them, and probably carried them with him into exile. I am also disposed to think that he rewrote and perhaps embellished them, adding here and there a word of explanation. Quite likely he was inspired to enlarge the first portions and to incorporate some things which he learned from Jethro. But however much or little his revision, as we are not told of an appointed successor to Judah as the Scribe of the Tribes, it is to Moses, as an authorized agent, that the Book was early attributed; from him it was received by Israel, after his Divine commission as the leader and lawgiver of his people. The supernatural and the inspired are woven into its texture; Divine revelations and family events compose its substance, the Book being an Eclectic History of the early ages of mankind and a Contemporary History of the Chosen People. For Abraham wrote his chapters, not for the children of Lot, nor for the children of Nahor, but for the seed of Isaac; Isaac wrote not for Esau, nor for Ishmael, but for Jacob; Jacob wrote for his sons; while Judah wrote for Israel, and Moses wrote and revised for Israel and the world.

After the death of Moses and of Joshua the tribe

of Judah takes its appointed place as leader of Israel: They asked of the LORD, Who shall go up for us first against the Canaanites? And the LORD said, Judah shall go up; behold, I have delivered the land into his hand (Judges 1 : 1, 2). Moreover, after the rejection of Saul, who was of the tribe of Benjamin, David, of the tribe of Judah, was anointed King. And notwithstanding the Disruption of the Kingdom under his grandson, the family of David continued to reign down to, if not, indeed, long after the Captivity. The sceptre did not really depart from Judah till Messiah came.

The *Book of Jasher* (62 : 23) records the death of Judah when one hundred and twenty-nine years old, and that he was embalmed, and put in a coffin, and given into the hands of his children. It was an honor done to his father and to Joseph, and marks Judah above his other brethren. The tradition is significant.

§ XVI.—*Conclusion.*

Now, if it be asked what is gained by adopting the proposed authorship thus presented, I answer with St. Paul, Much, every way. It removes root and branch the guesses of Kuenenism, Wellhausenism, and the rhetoric of Renan. Genesis and the Pentateuch cannot be ascribed to a human origin and development. The first Biblical book thus becomes true history, so far as it is history; true science for that age, so far as it treats of scientific matters, and a true Revelation from God touching all matters above human knowledge, whether of celestial beings, or of Divine covenant, or of special providences in first saving a doomed world, and then in preparation for the Redeemer of mankind. The *uniqueness* of the covenant with Abraham stamps its Divine origin.

Neither he nor any other man then could have devised and thought it out. He had travelled twelve hundred miles, had settled almost alone among strangers, had acknowledged the God El-Elyon of Melchizedek, and had paid him tithes. He was the first missionary of the world. It was a novel way to found a new nation and a new religion. He certainly had no scheme in his mind like other founders in later times, like Buddha or Mahomet. The setting up of a new religious cult was at first the farthest from his intention. Not till he was ninety-nine years old did he receive the seal of circumcision, the blood of which typified its value, being the symbol of life and the appointed means for covering sin. That was not Abraham's, but Jehovah's method. So when the system was completed under Moses, blood was the symbol which atoned for the sin of man. In old Canaan and at Sinai blood was the seal of Divine covenant. It was not Abraham, nor Moses, but God who appointed it to be so. The symbol of life was Jehovah's symbol of forgiveness. In Abel's sacrifice and at Moriah it was disclosed how atonement for sin could be obtained.

Moreover, the blood of circumcision linked and connected itself with the blood of the Passover-lamb. The blood of a lamb and the blood of man, centuries apart in time, was made the symbol of the Divine acceptance of the sinner. But while the significance was alike in each era, the plan was beyond the comprehension of Abraham and of Moses. Neither of them could have devised such a method, which is proof of its revelation. It was Heaven ordained.

The records also disclose unity and completeness. In the genealogy before the Deluge we find the heads of ten families, from Adam to Noah; though there may have been more, ten are mentioned. So in the genealogy of Abraham, ten heads of families trace him back to Shem. It is the number of completeness. A list of ten progenitors traces him up to Shem, and another list of ten traces him up from Noah to Adam.

For suppose it can be shown, as Dr. Winchell and others have attempted, that other beings like man once occupied this earth, yet the records of Noah's family and of Abraham's show their descent in direct line from Adam, who was God-created. And the law of Deuteronomy 23 : 2, 3 was in fact observed. Lot's children, Ammon and Moab, could not enter the assembly of Jehovah unto the tenth generation, for all future ages. While the records of Noah, of Abraham, and of Moses testify to the purity of Israel's descent for twice ten generations in regular succession. It is a very ancient example of the importance of family purity, of family descent, and of contemporary records.

This explains the great care afterward seen in preserving the genealogy of the Hebrews. One-third of the I Chronicles is occupied with tables of descent. It is seen in Ezra 2 : 61, 62 in a remarkable ruling which excluded certain claimants from the priest's office, because of mixed marriages. Compare Neh. 7 : 63, 64. Descendants of Barzillai, the Gileadite, were thus rejected. But a rule which had been operative from time immemorial, from Abraham to Moses, to David and Ezra, must have been believed to be of Divine appointment. It was before the Law of Sinai, and is another illustration of very early records. The rule is found back of Ezra, back of Moses, and has its roots in the ten generations of Abraham and the ten generations of Noah.

As moderns have their correspondents the world over, so the ancient leaders of Egypt and the Orient had their scribes, who recorded their achievements. Thus Sneferu and Sargon and the early Pharaohs inscribed their deeds, and perhaps an image of themselves on the rocks of the Wady Magharah, or of Cyprus, or on some obelisk or temple. But the Patriarchs built an altar, or married a wife, or dug a well, or made a treaty, and then wrote an account of their doings in the register of the Tribes, and so preserved the record for their descendants. Especially careful were they in all matters concerning Divine covenant and their relations to it and to God. Hence the early writing of Genesis.

Perhaps too much is said about European scepticism, and calling this Old Testament book and that New Testament book legendary and mythical, written when and by whom nobody knows! It is alike destructive of Christian belief and of Christian growth. First, the *difficulties* of Revelation are magnified, and then the Scriptures are rejected because of those difficulties!

The truth and strength of my argument find support in the evidence for very early writing as attested by the inscriptions of Babylonia and Egypt. It is conceded by M. Renan, who meets it in the weakest possible way—viz., by suggesting that the discoveries of Tel-el-Amarna are forgeries! To forge a record which nobody living could write is not yet among our modern achievements. But the argument here presented, as well as that in " Bible Growth and Religion," does not depend on the Tel-el-Amarna inscriptions, nor upon the statue of Rameses II., found at Bubastis, from which Rameses had erased the name of a Hyksos king and inscribed his own instead; nor upon the mummy of Sekenen-Ra, of Thebes, showing that his skull had been cloven through, causing his death, probably while fighting against the Hyksos. I say, my argument does not depend upon these disclosures, though they tend to strengthen it. We go back of

Rameses II. and Sekenen-Ra to the inscriptions of the twelfth dynasty; to the Hittite writing of Hebron and Zoan; to the illustrations of Syrian visitors in Egypt; to the inscriptions upon the obelisks, in the tombs, upon early temples and pyramids; to records of the fourth dynasty, of the second dynasty, and, according to Professor Sayce, of the first dynasty. We find the inscriptions of Sargon I. and of his son, of Khammuragas, of Kuder-Mabug and Arioch mentioned in Gen. 14, and the artistic skill mentioned in Gen. 4 : 19–22.

The rocks of Cyprus and of Sinai, the inscriptions of Babylon concerning Marduk, the Messiah, and of Istar weeping for Tammuz, like Eve for Abel, are not forgeries. Nor are the stone cylinders now in the British Museum which represent a man and a woman in the act of plucking fruit from a tree, and a serpent erect standing behind the woman. Nor is the inscription about the scorpion-men, the cherubim-like guardians of the way to the tree of life and to Eden itself, translated in June, 1889, by Mr. Boscawen. Nor is there any doubt of the legends and their meaning, which we call Deluge Legends in Chaldea, with their confirmation in Egypt, India, and China. Their account agrees substantially with our Genesis, and with the arts named in Gen. 4 disclose a degree of skill which implies the ability to read and write. How else was preserved the record of the ten Adamic generations down to Noah, and of the ten generations from Noah to Abraham? And as " probability is the very guide of life," we have the very great probability which the records disclose that Abraham and his successors wrote the Genesis which was early studied, and later revised by Moses. This accounts for all peculiarities of style and language.

It is a sufficient answer to all modern analysts of the text of our Genesis, and is as probable as the literature of Babylonia and Egypt can make it. The forgery of those literatures is impossible, while their existence in the days of Abraham and his sons all but demonstrates the patriarchs as writing memoirs of their times.

In the name of Him who gave the Revelation in our Genesis, I entreat the reader, both of the critical and the traditional school, to pause and reconsider my suggestions before relegating them among the theories which *may* be true. Patriarchal writing honors reason, explains conceded difficulties, and enthrones God in the Book of Genesis. If used as a provisional basis of exposition, and tested by experience, the unfoldings of the future will best determine whether acceptance shall be final and satisfactory.

II.

INTERNAL EVIDENCE FOR AN EARLY WRITER OF ISAIAH 40-66.

ALL critics, we are told, concede a similarity of style in the last twenty-seven chapters of Isaiah with that of the first forty chapters. And similar technical expressions are common in each division; for example, "The Holy One of Israel" and "The Servant of Jehovah." Similar Hymns are common to both sections of the Prophecies, while there is a noticeable infrequency of "visions;" thus chapter 6 in the first division and chapter 63 in the second part stand alone.

Ancient tradition, the Jewish Synagogue, Eccles. 48 : 24, 25, quotations by the later prophets, by Josephus, and by early Christian writers, as well as its long-time place in the Canon, all attribute the Book of Isaiah to one and the same Author. The purpose of this inquiry, however, is not the unity of its authorship, but its comparatively early date. Prophecies of the highest order, stirring exhortations, and very remarkable history are common to both sections. By examining portions of the last twenty-seven chapters, we expect to find an approximate date for the writing.

In chapter 40 : 18-26 we have the demand, "To whom will ye liken God? or what likeness will ye compare unto Him? The graven image, a workman melted it, and the goldsmith spreadeth it over with gold, and casteth for it silver chains." Then follows a grand description of Jehovah's power, who again demands, "To whom then will ye liken Me? Lift up your eyes on high, and see who hath created these heavenly things, calling them all by name . . . not one is lacking."

Now, whoever cannot appreciate the force of the prophet's argument and the grandeur of his language of course cannot see the utter absurdity of such deliverances in Palestine at any time after the destruction of Jerusalem in 586 B.C., when idolatry ceased there, or of an Exile Jew so addressing the Assyrian or Babylonian Gentile. For the Jew it was too late; for the Gentile it was a century too early. Even if the writer of these chapters was authenticated by the Prophet Jeremiah, since he died in about 572 B.C., it would be singularly absurd to make such a comparison of Jehovah with graven images at that time; for none remained in the ruined city of Zion; only the poorest of the people were left; and Gentiles were jubilant victors, not disposed to regard those who derided their deities. Nebuchadnezzar effected a large clearance in Judæa. So a prophet of the LORD would not stultify himself by exhorting to forsake the worship of graven images from 586 to 570 B.C., nor, perhaps, till after Cyrus took Babylon.

I have tried repeatedly to apply the comforting character and the shepherding character disclosed in chapter 40 to Cyrus, but in vain; he never approaches the standard, and there was little of the herald of good tidings about him. He was as astute a politician as an accomplished soldier, but preacher of righteousness and the worship of Israel's God he was not in any such way or degree as to fulfil the description in chapter 40. The Church appoints the reading of the first eleven verses for St. John Baptist Day, which suggests her opinion of their interpretation.

Compare Jer., chapters 10, 50, 51, which, however, were written before their fulfilment. The great similarity in the contents is conclusive for an early date of the Isaianic passages. Thus, touching idolatry we read, "Behold, their works are vanity and nought: their molten images are wind and confusion" (Is. 41 : 29). I invite the critics to prove that this passage was not written before the Fall of Jerusalem, in 586. After that date prophets had no occasion to denounce idolatry in Judæa. But see the accentuation of it in chapter 42 : 8, " I am Jehovah ; . . . my glory will I not give to another, neither my praise unto graven images." And verse 24 asks, " Who gave Jacob for a spoil, and Israel to the robbers? did not Jehovah?"

This is a time-mark, and shows the passage was written after the capture of Samaria by Sargon II., when Jacob was spoiled and Israel robbed, but before the capture of Jerusalem by Nebuchadnezzar— *i.e.*, some time between 721 and 586 B.C. These dates are as well defined as that of our American Independence. With 586 idolatry ceased in Judæa, and no writer like the author of 42 : 17 would denounce the "trust in graven images, and the invocation of molten images." If the writer is supposed to have lived in Babylonia, he would not dare to denounce the idolatry of Babylonians. But put the deliverance of the text before 586, and all is easy of exposition. An inspired writer explains what even a truthful historian leaves inexplicable. Hence, I prefer the one miracle of prophecy to the manifold confusions arising from assigning it to a later date.

So, again, in chapter 43 : 1, 3, it implies that Jehovah had given Egypt, Ethiopia, and Seba as a ransom for Jacob and Israel ; which could have no meaning after the Fall of the Holy City. Verse 14 is against Babylon and the Chaldeans, and verse 28 "will profane the sanctuary, and make Jacob a curse and Israel a reviling ;" showing that the curse and the reproach were yet to be—viz., before 586 B.C.

In chapter 44 : 1-8 is a detailed promise of help and blessing, followed by an exaltation of Jehovah's supremacy, which was not required to be stated after the Restoration under Cyrus ; yet in verses

9-20 are "the carpenter's description and the baker's description of making a god of wood, and then burning the chips in order to bake bread therewith, or to warm one's self at the fire thereof," which would have no relevancy if uttered after 586 B.C.; for the Hebrews were cured of idolatry in Babylonia.

Moreover, the conditions of pardon and restoration, unfolded in 44 : 21–45 : 25 are prophetic; for the comparison of Jehovah with the gods of the nations is continued, even to "the wood of their graven images, and prayer unto a god that cannot save" (45 : 20, 21). This had no application to Cyrus, who accepted the doctrine of Two eternal Principles of Good and Evil, and he was not a worshipper of images. His attendance upon the sacrifices in Babylonian temples disclosed his tolerance, or, if you prefer, his indifferentism to national religions. He certainly granted favors to the Hebrew exiles, and by decree provided for their return, and the restoration of all their sacred things. But his favor to them did not incite him to attack the shrines of Babylon. Not yet did Bel fall or Nebo crouch to the conqueror. Not yet "shall they go into confusion together that are makers of idols" (45 : 16). But Judah was to follow Ephraim into exile. So it came to pass; the Kingdom of the South also became captive. "All Israel, all the ends of the earth, shall be saved by looking unto God. In Jehovah shall all the seed of Israel be justified, and shall glory." It was then to be (45 : 22-25).

Not only is the nation's deliverer named, and the terms of Pardon and Restoration stated for Judah and Ephraim, but the supremacy of Jehovah is insisted upon for Jew and for Gentile. After how long an interval is not said, but it is affirmed as a fact to be accomplished (chapter 46 : 1), as Schrader tersely renders, "Bel sinks, Nebo falls down." And the Revised Version, "Their idols are upon the beasts, and upon the cattle ; themselves are gone into captivity" (verses 1, 2). It sounds like prophetic ridicule : Bel and Nebo are taken prisoners. Orelli places this under Artaxerxes, but Herodotus, P. Smith, Rawlinson, and Professor Sayce place it under Xerxes I., at least forty years after Cyrus, but probably before he entered upon the war against Greece. Herodotus (Book 1, chapter 183) says : " Xerxes took away the golden image of Bel, and killed the priest who forbade him to move the statue." This, I presume, was before the war with Greece, and Xerxes actually seized the statues of Bel and of Nebo, and coined them into money, to aid in his campaign against Greece. Then, after his return, he destroyed the temple of Belus, so Arrian (vii. 17). Xerxes would hardly have done so provoking a thing before that war, lest it fomented worse evils than seemed pending, but upon his return his resentment was intensified by his defeat.

It was Nebuchadnezzar, after the devastations of Sennacherib, that rebuilt Bel's temple and replaced the silver image, which he overlaid with plates of gold, and enriched his worship. Indeed, no son could do more honor to his father and show more love for him than Nebuchadnezzar showed to Bel Merodach. He entered his temple, took him by the hand, and thanked him for his blessings and his triumphs. He adored him at great cost. This temple continued to Xerxes I., when he pillaged and then destroyed the temple of Bel and of Nebo. Their worship, however, held on, with various fortune, to the third or fourth Christian century. (So Rawlinson's "Herodotus," 4th ed., London, vol. i., pp. 660-668.) But the words of the prophet were fulfilled when, in about 485 B.C., a full century after the Fall of Jerusalem, Bel and Nebo were captured by the Persian king and converted to his own uses by being coined into money for his wars against the Greeks.

Dr. Cheyne seems to regard the passage as written of Cyrus, and that the conqueror disappointed prophetic expectations when he tolerated and did not destroy the worship of Bel and of Nebo. But surely 46 : 1 and 2 may have no reference to Cyrus, but only to him who, like Xerxes, made those images to vanish from before him! As a successor of Cyrus and the avenger of Jehovah upon idols Xerxes I. seems to have fulfilled all the requirements of the prophecy. It recalls the irony of Elijah against the dupes of Baal (1 Kings 18). But while he was laughing at the idolaters of Israel, the writer of Is. 46 : 1-2 portrays, before the event, the helplessness and capture of the Babylonian idols. He also further insists upon the supremacy and sovereignty of Jehovah (verses 3-13). It was prophecy not yet fulfilled.

Those who make history of it ignore 47 : 1-7 : "Come down, and sit in the dust, O virgin daughter of Babylon ; sit on the ground without a throne, O daughter of the Chaldeans ! I will take vengeance, and will accept no man as a truce maker between us. Get thee into darkness, O daughter of the Chaldeans ! Two things shall come upon thee in one day, the loss of children, and widowhood ; there shall be none to save thee" (verses 9, 15). These predictive utterances were literally fulfilled at Babylon by Cyrus in 538. Belshazzar was slain, and his father, Nabonidus, died soon after. The country, like that of Israel and Judah, was bereft of both her kings. In little more than half a century Bel and Nebo were melted into current coin. We cannot bring these several events nearer together. There is the discussion against idolatry, the word about Cyrus, about Bel and Nebo ; in 66 : 6 a word goes forth from the temple ; no one human life could span those 215 years, or from the siege of Sennacherib to the capture of Xerxes I. To reduce the prophetic portraiture which we find in chapters 44 to 48 to a history of occurrences is to do violence to the text, its time-marks, and its arguments. It ignores the *futures* in 48 : 14, 20, " Shall perform His pleasure on Babylon : Go ye forth of Babylon, flee ye from the Chaldeans, tell it to the ends of the earth !" Surely this, when spoken, had not been done? Bel Merodach had not fallen and Nebo had not prostrated himself before the God of gods.

Hence, the actual fall of those false gods was a striking confirmation of the predictions and contrasts in Is. 40-46, and of Jer. 10, 50, 51. But Isaiah is never more sure of the Restoration of Judah than was Jeremiah, who, when in prison, sent his servant to purchase the field, whose right of redemption was his, saying : " Thus saith Jehovah, God of Israel : Houses, and fields, and vineyards shall be possessed again in this land." Compare Jer. 32 : 2-15 ; 36 to 44 with Is. 48 : 12-20 ; 49 : 8-26. So the writer of these portions of Isaiah is corroborated by Jeremiah, and he again by Micah. The predictions of each are alike explicit. Compare Jer. 15th chapter. Also what is said of a certain Roman who, after the disaster at Cannæ, bought a piece of the ground then occupied by Hannibal. No ; the accuracy of a fulfilment of prophecy does not prove it false, nor that it was written after the events.

Moreover, chapter 49 informs us that the isles of Japheth shall see the exaltation and return of Jacob, even as they saw his humiliation and captivity.

Verses 25, 26 could scarcely be more expressive of deliverance: "Thus saith Jehovah, Even the captives of the mighty shall be taken away, and the prey of the terrible shall be delivered; for I will contend with him that contendeth with thee, and I will save thy children. And I will feed them that oppress thee with their own flesh; and they shall be drunken with their own blood, as with sweet wine: and all flesh shall know that I, the LORD, am the Saviour and thy Redeemer, the Mighty One of Jacob." All this was in the future when the prophet wrote, and when Jeremiah wrote, but found its accomplishment in the conspiracy of the priests against Nabonidus for not being more devoted to them, and they prepared the way for Cyrus by conspiracy against the government, so that Belshazzar and others fell by the hand of the assassins among their own Babylonians, rather than by the sword of the Persians. This is the revised history of the Fall of Babylon. Her people were drunk with their own blood, through the slaughter of conspirators, and in 538 B.C. fulfilled Is. 49 : 26. But 46 : 1 was fulfilled by Xerxes I. rather more than fifty years later.

The divorcement mentioned in chapter 50 : 1, 2 may be better applied to the Ten Tribes already in Exile than to Judah, for whose transgression the mother was put away when the larger part of Israel was carried captive. But the sin of both kingdoms now left them without a man to deliver them; only

Jehovah could redeem and save them; so the prophet describes Him (verses 2-11). The description is grandly continued in predictive poetry through chapter 51, and to verse 13 of chapter 52. The language is very thrilling. Whether the " Awake, awake, put on strength, O arm of Jehovah"— " Awake, awake, stand up, O Jerusalem"— " Awake, awake, put on thy strength, O Zion; put on thy beautiful garments, O Jerusalem, the holy city!" a city then laid waste, as some say—whether these exhortations were uttered by the prophet through inspired vision of future unfoldings, or were the deliverances of a later herald, must be determined by the light already shed upon our theme and by what may yet dawn. Certain it is they preceded the return from Babylon, and did not receive complete fulfilment under Cyrus. A diviner Light should yet arise for Judah.

We may find another time mark in 52 : 4, 5, " Saith the LORD God, My people went down at the first to sojourn in Egypt," they did not expect to abide there, but were kept for some centuries. Leaping over other centuries, " The Assyrian oppressed them without cause." That is, Shalmaneser IV. and Sargon II. had no grievance to avenge for which to invade Israel and carry Samaria captive. " Now, therefore, saith Jehovah, seeing my people is taken away for nought, and their rulers make them howl, and my name is continually blasphemed" (through the honors paid to Bel and

Nebo), "Therefore my people shall know my name, and that I am here to speak for them; behold, it is I." I have adopted the margin of the Revised Version in verse 6.

The prophet here states that neither Israel nor Judah had wronged Assyria and Babylon, who were, therefore, to be punished for their offences committed while chastizing the Hebrews for their sins against God. The eternal law of righteousness is regnant and illustrated, and also the Divine promise to Abraham. His heritage was Canaan, and it passed to Israel. They sought refuge from famine in Egypt, and were kept there for centuries. They were not captives, but detained and enslaved till Jehovah delivered them. Later on they were captured by force of arms, and carried now into Assyria and now to Babylonia. It was not, like the going down to Egypt, a voluntary migration, but a seizure. Longer detention there would interfere with the Divine plan of man's Redemption; break the promise to Abraham, and let the Gentile blaspheme. Hence Judah was to be rescued and restored, and the oppressor chastized. The exiles were exhorted to "look unto Abraham, their father, and unto Sarah, their mother: in unity he had been called and blessed, and of one made many. Jehovah will comfort Zion, and make her deserts like Eden. Joy and gladness shall be found therein, thanksgiving, and the voice of melody" (51 : 2, 3 ; 52 : 3-6).

National deliverance is coupled with the world's

salvation; the prophet describes the suffering Messiah, who becomes an offering for sin, bearing the iniquities of others, and making intercession for the people (chapter 52 : 13-53 : 12). Surely, if this passage of a suffering Saviour for Israel is in its proper place here, there are connected two related subjects —viz., the salvation of Israel and salvation by the Christ. Chapter 53 : 4-12 cannot be adequately explained of any Deliverer from national exile ; for He is a Sufferer, and suffers the full penalty in His own person for the transgressions of others. He is not like Moses, who led forth his people from Egypt ; nor like David, who delivered them from the power of the Philistines ; nor like Hezekiah, who went into the Temple, and with the letter of Sennacherib spread before Jehovah, besought Him to rescue His people from the besieging army. Those deliverers suffered no penalty ; but this righteous Servant justifies and delivers many, by bearing their iniquities Himself, by the travail of His own soul (verse 11).

Throughout these connected chapters we find a complex, dual subject : there are the supremacy of Jehovah and exposure of the absurdity of idols and idol worship; the warnings and denunciations against sin and the threatened judgments upon it ; predicted exile and promised restoration. The penalty follows transgression. Jehovah triumphs over all rival deities ; Bel and Nebo bow before Him. For the salvation of the world, a captive nation shall be delivered from captivity and be re-established in their own land. For the God of Abraham had promised to keep the covenant made with him for blessing mankind.

Filled with these assurances of the deliverance of Jehovah's people—barren, desolate, and forsaken, like a deserted wife, as they then were—the writer breaks forth into the highest strains of poetry: "Sing, O barren, thou that didst not bear. Thou shalt be enlarged, and shalt possess the nations. As the Flood of Noah abated, and the earth was renewed, so Jehovah will renew His promises to His people. His covenant of peace, of which the enduring mountains were witness, should not be broken, but His kindness should return to them, and God would gather them with great mercies" (54 : 1-10). Then another prophetic hymn was followed by a personal invitation to "Every one that thirsteth to come to the waters; to come freely, without money, and partake of wine and milk without cost. For Jehovah, God of Israel, would glorify them" (55 : 1-5). But this was never true of the national restoration; that was at great cost to Persian princes and to the returned Hebrews. The prophet therefore looked forward to the preaching of the Messiah. (Compare St. Matt. 11 : 28-30.)

In Isaiah 55 : 6-13 the subjective conditions, prayer, penitence, righteousness, are described and enjoined. Purity and loyalty are required of men, because God is highly exalted above all the earth.

Even the natural world testified to His supremacy, and that He would cause fir-trees and myrtle-trees to take the place of thorns and briers, as an everlasting sign of His faithfulness. The redemption of His people would be accompanied by the glad acclaim of mountains and hills, and the trees of the field would clap their hands. This, of course, is poetry, but it is poetry inspired. It is Jehovah speaking by His prophet. Why that prophet is not the same as he who wrote and sung the first five chapters of Isaiah is not discoverable from the text. The style, tone, and verbal expressions are much alike; only difference of subject seems to differentiate the writer. It is at least very probable that both of these sections were written before the Exile to Babylon. Compare chapters 10 and 11. Jerusalem is threatened (10 : 11), yet the dispersed of Judah will be gathered from the four corners of the earth (11 : 12).

If one should collate passages from the last twenty-seven chapters, and compare them with their parallels in the first forty chapters of Isaiah, and with Jeremiah, the absurdity of relegating the last twenty-seven chapters to a period *after* these two prophets would be manifest. Read carefully Jer. 13-15 chapters, where we find similar matter to that of Isaiah, "Line upon line, and precept upon precept." Such similarity does not indicate that the Second Isaiah was after the First, nor after Jeremiah. And some time marks suggest that he may have been between them—*e.g.* Is. 66 : 6, where the " Voice of the temple, with the tumult of the city, and the recompense upon Jehovah's enemies," point to Sennacherib's letter which Hezekiah then spread before the LORD (chapter 37 : 14–20). At no other time in that era, from 721–586 B.C., is the threefold voice to be heard. Not till this nineteenth century was there any serious doubt of its date. The section was translated into the Septuagint without question, was collated by Origen in the third century, and by Jerome in the fourth, without suspicion that those twenty-seven chapters were not prophecy as truly as the first forty chapters, as truly as the predictions of Jeremiah are prophecy. They are prophetic exhortations, warnings, songs, foreseeings, not written after the events.

The exhortation of chapter 55 is continued in 56 and in 57, while in 58 it is only more urgent : " Cry aloud, spare not, lift up thy voice like a trumpet, and declare unto My people their transgression, and to the house of Jacob their sins." It proceeds with conditional promises of pending blessings, yet as though Judah still observed her feasts and fasts in Jerusalem (verse 2). And the figure of "lifting up the voice like a trumpet," which was strikingly fitting in a city, or before a large assembly, has no meaning for a people scattered, captured, and exiled throughout the Assyrian empire. So of chapter 59 : " Will you shorten Jehovah's hand and dull His ear, so that He can neither hear nor save ? Is *truth so fallen in our streets,* and departed from us, that we are become a prey, and the righteous stand afar off, while our sins testify against us (verses 12, 14, 15)? Indeed, the whole chapter is an argument that *Jerusalem yet stands,* but is in peril through transgression ; that a redeemer shall come to Zion, and to the penitent in Jacob, saith Jehovah" (verse 20).

Moreover, the word Zion used of the Temple, and Jacob, used for Canaan, imply that the people were then at home and their beautiful house not then destroyed. Thus verses 16–19 have a stronger emphasis—" Oh, that one may interpose for us, that the Divine Arm may bring us salvation instead of vengeance ; then shall we of the west fear Jehovah, and His glory shall be seen from the rising of the sun. A redeemer shall come to Zion, and the Divine Spirit shall be upon them, and His words shall be in their mouth, and shall not depart out of their mouth, nor out of the mouth of their seed's seed, saith Jehovah, from henceforth and for ever" (verse 21). All this reads as much like conditional prophecy before its accomplishment as anything we find from Samuel to Malachi. Compare Mal. 2 : 17–3 : 7. The frequent iterations of conditional blessings and of penalties are as natural in the last section as in the first section of Isaiah. He cannot be changed into an historian and narrator of accomplished facts.

Nor can we explain the " Arise, shine ; for thy

light is come" of Cyrus, in 60 : 1, since the whole account of the wonders mentioned leads up to verse 22, " I, Jehovah, will hasten it in its time." But it was a conditional promise. The nations had not come to that light, nor their kings to the brightness of its rising. Nor had the wealth of the nations, the frankincense from Sheba, the flocks of Kedar, and the rams of Nebaioth yet glorified the house of the LORD at Jerusalem. From her predicted judgments after the capture of Samaria the people had not became righteous; though righteousness conditioned their possession of the land forever. But not yet had this promise been realized ; not yet had Jehovah hastened its advent.

In due course, however, Nebuchadnezzar acknowledged the Most High God as supreme in heaven and in earth ; Darius and Artaxerxes proclaimed Him ; while Xerxes I. carried off Bel and Nebo from Babylon, and destroyed the great temple there. Thenceforth on the Euphrates, as for more than a century on the Jordan, no remonstrances were needed against graven images. Nor would a prophet who could write like the author of Is. 40–66 stultify himself by denouncing a forsaken idolatry. The inference, therefore, must be that when he wrote idolatry was a crying sin in Judæa. It was *before* its extirpation by capture and by exile.

In chapter 61 : 1–10 the " Anointed One was promised to preach glad tidings to the poor, to bind up the broken-hearted, to proclaim liberty to the captives, the opening of prison doors, the acceptable year of Jehovah, and His day of vengeance ; also to comfort the mourners, meeting them in Zion, and changing their heaviness into joy and rejoicing : they should become the planted of the LORD, and He glorified in them. Former wastes were to be repaired, new priests were to be named, the covenant was to be renewed, and national renown secured." And to emphasize the assurance of all this the Spirit of the LORD descends upon the preacher to encourage devout seekers after Him. For reproach and confusion they shall repossess their lands and rejoice in their portion. As a bride and bridegroom, so should they adorn themselves and become a praise before all nations.

This is strongly accentuated to the penitent: " For Zion's sake will I not hold my peace, and for Jerusalem's I will not rest, until her righteousness go forth as brightness, and her salvation as a lamp that burneth. . . And thou shalt be called by a new name—viz., Beulah : for Jehovah delighteth in thee, and thy land shall be married. . . Thou shalt be a crown of beauty and a royal diadem in the hand of the LORD thy God" (62 : 1–5). These promises of glory and blessedness are continued throughout the chapter. It describes the watchman of Jehovah, and His sworn pledge to Jerusalem : her sanctuary shall be honored by those who gathered and garnered her people's harvests. So it came to pass under Persian kings : " Say ye to the

6

daughter of Zion, Behold, thy salvation cometh; behold, his reward is with him, and his recompense before him." This cannot be said of Cyrus. Yet the holy people, "the redeemed of the LORD, shall be called, sought out, a city not forsaken" (verses 6-12).

As did other prophets, as did our Lord, the writer here blends and connects the deliverer of Israel from captivity with the Redeemer of the world, who should tread the winepress alone for its salvation; it was the grand symbolization of Redemption. To call it a rhetorical statement of facts may leave us its poetry, but poetry without meaning. As mere history, its point and essence evaporate. The traveller from Edom, with crimsoned garments, described in chapter 63, is far more than a gloriously apparelled prince: "He is strong, He is righteous, mighty to save: His garments are sprinkled with lifeblood. He looked, and there was none to help; therefore His arm brought salvation; He trode down the peoples in anger, made them drunk in his fury, and poured out their lifeblood on the earth" (verses 1-6). Even if this can be said of Cyrus, the rest of the chapter cannot be so applied—viz., the praises of Jehovah and His mercies; the rebellion of the people and their affliction; the Angel of his presence who saved them, the love and pity that redeemed Israel; that bare them, and carried them all the days of old; the reference to Moses and his works, dividing the water and lead-ing his people through the depths ; the prayer for the return of the Tribes, so passionately implored in verse 17—all this is without meaning as applied to Cyrus, and it was not fulfilled in the Restoration under him. Nor is there any proper comparison between him and Moses in verse 11.

With verse 18, and continuing to the end of chapter 64, is a different treatment of a similar theme. The holy people are said to have possessed their heritage but a little while, when their adversaries trode down the sanctuary, and they became as though God never bare rule over them, and they were not called by His name. These conditions did not exist under the Persian kings, unless applicable to the evils wrought by Sanballet and Tobiah, exaggerated reports of which may have come to some prophet of the Exile ; and hence this passionate appeal to Jehovah : Oh, that He would rend the heavens, let the mountains burn, that He would descend as upon Sinai, and make the nations tremble at His presence ! The language is too strong to be spoken of relief from any local distress in Judæa during the Persian supremacy. It must belong to the era just before the destruction by Babylon, or look forward to the troubles under Antiochus Epiphanes, or under Titus and the Romans. And the writer proceeds with historic allusions to God's terribleness, that He requires loyalty, recognizing none besides Him ; how He meeteth the doer of righteousness ; how He was wroth against sinners ; how

He would pardon their iniquities, and restore their beautiful house, then represented as desolate and burned with fire. The last point may be a prophetic time mark, showing it was uttered before 586 B.C. It certainly was not said of accomplished promises to gather captives already returned! Verses 10 and 11 prove that.

Must it not be considered in relation with the idolatry denounced in chapter 44? "Be not wroth very sore, O Lord, neither remember iniquity for ever. Thou art our Father" (64 : 8, 9). Compare 44 : 21-24. Yet as sure as that the Hebrew exiles did not worship graven images in Babylon, of which Daniel and his friends are examples, so sure the temple was not burned nor Jerusalem a desolation when 44 : 6-20 was written. Indeed, I prefer to regard chapter 64 as a work of Daniel, related to Dan. 9 : 1-19, which has been misplaced by some copyist of the time of Ezra, and so fitted in where we find it, than to relegate the second grand division of Isaiah to a period after the destruction of city and temple by Nebuchadnezzar. Or we may consider it a prayer of Ezekiel, following Ezek. 39 : 29, which has been misplaced; or the effusion of some other prophet before the Restoration, rather than allow it to drag its now connected chapters to a time when they lose their meaning. It was certainly written before Cyrus, and so is not history. Yet, as is tersely said, " A word of history is worth a mountain of theory"—a rule to be applied to the exposition of prophecy. But some are so misled by a theory, now touching prophecy, now legislation, now the development of theology in Israel, and now to make history of a Second Isaiah, that they ignore contemporary facts and records which illustrate this period of the Hebrews, and so they cannot interpret Hebrew prophecy aright.

However my suggestion may be regarded by those competent to judge, I am free to confess that Is. 64 seems to be a prayer prophecy, uttered when Judah was in Exile and her temple in ruins ; uttered before her return and before the restoration of Zion. It is not an interpolation for a purpose, but a reverent misplacement of a passage, when such misplacement was easy. But it was before Cyrus that Jehovah was invoked to rend the heavens, shake the mountains, and make His name terrible to the nations, even as He appeared at Sinai (64 : 1, 2).

My suggestion, therefore, connects 63 : 17 with 65 : 1. Thus the related passages of a Suffering Messiah who delivers Israel and redeems the world, are linked to that which makes Him inquired after by those who sought Him not ; first by the Persians and later by the Greeks. They fit well together. Then the writer returns to treat of Judah, when her people wrought abomination and were rebellious : sacrificing in gardens, burning incense upon bricks, eating swine's flesh and broth of abominable things ; they were idolaters, yet conspicuous for their self-righteousness. "I will recompense into their bosom, saith Jehovah, them that have burned incense upon the mountains, and blasphemed, or defied me upon the hills: I will measure their work into their bosom" (verses 2-7). Yet because of the loyal and faithful among them, a seed of Jacob and of Judah shall inherit the good land promised to their fathers. Sharon and Achor shall pasture their flocks; but they who follow Fortune and Destiny as gods shall fall by the sword; because when the Lord called they would not regard it (65 : 8-12).

It suggests what St. Paul says of the rejection of the Jew and the calling of the Gentile, that Israel may be saved. The old leaven of truth remaining among them shall lead to their rehabilitation. God will create Jerusalem a rejoicing, and her people a joy; He will rejoice in them. They shall reap the fruit of their labors and dwell in their own houses. Jehovah will anticipate their needs, and hear before they call. Even the brute creation shall be blessed: the wolf and the lamb, the lion and the ox, shall be companions. The serpent shall not hurt, none shall destroy in the holy mountain, saith the Lord (65 : 13-25). For, behold, "I create new heavens and a new earth." Historically, this has not been fulfilled. It seems to anticipate the triumph of the principles unfolded in the Sermon on the Mount. But even then children may die, and old men before reaching a century of years. The new creation, however, is shown to be a conditional renovation for Jerusalem and her people, but it was a condition which they never realized, because of their disobedience.

Chapter 66 begins to correct the material prosperity which was erroneously expected from the passage commencing at verse 17 of chapter 65. The new dispensation to be introduced by Him whose throne is heaven, and whose footstool the earth, will need no temple like that which Solomon built; for the Most High dwelleth not in temples made with hands; neither is worshipped as though He needed anything (Acts 17 : 24, 25); what sort of house will ye build for Him? and where shall He be located? His own hand hath made all things, saith Jehovah. Then the new creation is described as the Lord dwelling in the heart of a poor and contrite man, who trembles at His word, by anxiety to obey it. Thus our Lord in St. John 4 : 24, "God is a Spirit; and they that worship Him must worship Him in spirit and in truth." He needs no temple of mechanical design and workmanship, but is content to abide in the hearts of His faithful people.

This new and spiritual teaching is then illustrated by the prophet's comparison of it with the former system wherein material acts were of chief importance; but under the new system, the cruelty of killing an ox is likened to the slaying of a man; the sacrificing a lamb to breaking the neck of a dog; the offering an oblation was defilement like offering swine's blood: even to burn incense was materialism like idolatry. Yet this people "choose their own methods, and their soul delighteth in their abominations." They do not accept what I have offered them. "I also will choose their delusions, and will bring their fears upon them; because when I called none did answer; when I spake they did not hear; but they did that which was evil in mine eyes, and chose that wherein I delighted not." The reader will now see how utterly different is this part of the prophet's discourse from much that has preceded it. He has leaped beyond the Jerusalem temple, beyond Judæa, to have his Lord found of them who sought Him not. The reference is back to chapter 65, where Persians and Greeks and other Gentiles—nations not called by the Divine name—now inquire for Jehovah and the new covenant which He has made with man. This new dispensation has nothing to do with Cyrus, nor with anything he did, or failed to do, for Israel, Israel the called and the rejected.

Another matter is connected with it for those who hear the Lord's word: "Your brethren that hated you, that cast you out for My name's sake, have said, Let Jehovah be glorified, that we may see your joy; but they shall be ashamed." We, your brethren of Ephraim, have seen Baal fall in Samaria; let us see your joy. No, you shall be ashamed! What, says the prophet, do you not remember the "voice of tumult from the city," when Sennacherib besieged it with his 200,000 men, and the "voice of prayer from the temple," when Hezekiah spread his blasphemous letter before Jehovah, and the voice which told that He would be avenged upon His enemies and deliver His people? Even before they suffered from the siege they were delivered. Not an arrow was shot at them, not a drop of their blood was shed before deliverance came to Jerusalem. The blatant boasters heard a rumor and escaped as fast as possible. They were utterly discomfited. Before the pain of travail, because of the siege, came upon the city the siege was raised, and the invaders fled away. Jerusalem rejoiced, and all that loved her also rejoiced. Baal had fallen, but Jehovah had triumphed. Those of Ephraim who saw it were ashamed, but Judah rejoiced.

This, I suggest, may be the exposition of 66 : 6-10. It meets all the points named in the text. Every element is verified, every requirement answered; even the figurative comparison is accounted for in each particular. The conditional element does not here exist. When the prophet wrote it was recent history, and it is a time mark of that fact. Of no other epoch is it applicable; not to Nebuchadnezzar, and he suffered no defeat; not to any later time of trouble in Jerusalem, or of the rebuilding of Zion. All the conditions find their verification when the Assyrian sent his defiant message to King Hezekiah, and he spread it before the LORD in the temple. Compare Nebuchadnezzar before Bel Merodach. Jehovah triumphed, for the cause was really His. And that wonderful deliverance, which the writer compares to an easy accouchement of the daughter of Zion, made a deep impression upon the people. It was the talk of the city.

With this grand event in mind the prophet gives assurance of the final deliverance of Judah from all her foes, and from all her sins. Her peace shall be like a river, and all her wants shall be satisfied. As one whom his mother comforteth, so will Jehovah comfort her, and she shall be comforted in Jerusalem (66 : 10–14). Sennacherib had defied the LORD; had compared the gods of even conquered nations to Him. Wherefore Tarshish, Pul, Lud, Tubal, Javan, and the isles afar off should hear of the fame and glory of Jehovah in rescuing His people. He would come with fire and sword, with chariots like a whirlwind, having great indignation against His enemies, and the slain of the LORD shall be many. Men must sanctify themselves and purify themselves from all idolatry, from eating swine's flesh and the mouse as a religious act, and offer a pure offering in the holy mountain Jerusalem, saith Jehovah, even as Israel bring their offering in a clean vessel into the house of the LORD. And of the Gentiles will He take for priests and for Levites. But when? Clearly, as in verse 22, when Jehovah makes the new heavens and the new earth—*i.e.*, when He establishes the new system of a more spiritual religion ; not when He has restored the Hebrews from captivity.

The writer, like St. Paul, leaps from theme to theme. Now he speaks of deliverance from the Assyrian, now of Jehovah in Jerusalem being mightier than Baal in Samaria, and of the comfort He gives to His people ; then he will have Jehovah glorified among the Gentiles, and they shall worship Him with pure offerings on Mount Zion—yea, the time cometh when He will take of them to be His priests and Levites. In verse 23 he indicates how and when the Gentiles—yea, all flesh, shall worship Him ; and they shall see the carcasses of the transgressors against Him (verse 24). So it came to pass.

The fulfilment of this prophecy was realized in part after the return from Exile. Cyrus, Darius, Artaxerxes, even Alexander the Great, all did honor to the God of the Hebrews. They restored their sacred things which had been captured, and their national privileges which had been forfeited. They made provision for rebuilding the temple and the resumption of its sacrifices, "that they may offer sacrifices of sweet savor unto the God of heaven, and pray for the life of the king, and of his sons." (See Ezra 6 : 1-12 ; 1 : 1-11.) Thus Jehovah was honored by Cyrus and by Darius. After that Artaxerxes ordered to teach those who knew not the laws of God (Ezra 7 : 25). How Alexander honored Him is stated in Josephus and briefly utilized in "Bible Growth and Religion," pp. 232, 233. How the opposition of Sanballet and Tobiah, mentioned in Neh. 2 : 10, was frustrated, we learn in the first part of that chapter. It, in fact, emphasizes the fostering care of three Persian kings, who, by decree and by deputy, fulfilled Is. 66 : 19 and 23. The reader should consult the references.

As in the destruction wrought by Assyrian, Babylonian, and Persian armies, all the threats of verses 15 and 16 were fulfilled, so in the rebuilding of Jerusalem and the restoration of the temple and its sacrifices under Cyrus, Darius, and Artaxerxes, all the nursing care promised in verses 10–14 found accomplishment. Even the "all flesh" of verse 23 was largely realized by the injunction of Darius, to "pray for the life of the king, and of his sons" in the daily service of the temple (Ezra 6 : 10). For then Darius represented the civilized world, except Greece ; Rome had not yet become a power ; and the successor of Cambyses as King of the Medes and Persians was also King of Babylonia and Assyria, of Syria and Judæa, of Egypt also, governing it by deputy.

Xerxes I. succeeded him, and fulfilled Isaiah 46 : 1, for he plundered the temple of Bel and other shrines at Babylon, and carried off their images, which he probably melted into money. They bowed and crouched before him in the coinage. Orelli says *Artaxerxes* carried off Bel and Nebo ; but according to Herodotus, who is sustained by Rawlinson, P. Smith, and later still by Professor Sayce, this was done by Xerxes I. about 485 B.C., when making his vast preparations for the war against Greece. Then he seized the treasures of Babylon, with their gods of gold and shrines of silver. It was a full century after the fall of Jerusalem. It is another authentication of prophecy. But it was done as a punishment upon a people who often rebelled against the Persian rule, and whose priests were made to suffer for their part in conspiring against the government and inviting Cyrus to become their chief. It was the priests of Babylon who compassed the overthrow of Nabonidus. They had excited the people against him ; they rebelled against the successors of Cyrus, and now Xerxes despoiled their temples, and left their priests without a sanctuary.

Thus the prophecy was fulfilled, even if a thorough clearance of idolatry from the country was not effected. For the Persians were not in the habit of interfering with the religion of subject peoples, unless their priests were suspected of fomenting discord, as in Babylon and in Egypt. With the Jews there was no religious opposition to the Persians, and their theology was singularly alike. Chapter 66 : 23 is also fulfilled, as is 19 : 19, by the erection of a temple like that at Jerusalem in Egypt. It was within the sanctuary of old Bubastis, where

Onias was permitted by the king to set up an altar to Jehovah, and there daily to celebrate a worship only a little less elaborate than that in the temple of Jerusalem. This continued in that old Egyptian nome Heliopolis, from 170 B.C. to 73 A.D., when it was destroyed by the Romans. See " Bible Growth and Religion," pp. 205, 233, 254, and Josephus *ad loc*. In the slaughter at Babylon by the conspiracy against Nabonidus, and the several punishments inflicted upon her for later rebellions, not to go as late as the conquest of Alexander, there was at least a measurable fulfilment of Is. 66 : 24.

Wherefore, to relegate this whole division of the work to a period which makes it history, and not prophecy, is a serious perversion of the text, a part of which refers to 701 B.C., and a part to Cyrus, a part to Darius in 519, his second year (Ezra 4 : 24), and a part to Xerxes in 485, and a part to Artaxerxes in his twentieth year, or about 445 B.C. As history it covers a period of 256 years; and, if from an unknown author, could not then have been admitted to a place with the earlier chapters of Isaiah. Its admission there certifies to its early writing.

I have shown the date of the fall of Bel and Nebo, and that no such writer as was the accomplished author of chapters 40–66 could write the denunciations against graven images contained in chapters 40, 44, and other passages *after* 586 B.C. I have conceded that 63 : 18–64 : 12 may be an unexplained misplacement of a later prophet. The comparison of Jehovah with graven images, and what is said of Bel and Nebo, of nursing kings for Judah, of Cyrus and the slain of the Lord, all this was years before the Restoration, before Darius requested prayers in Jerusalem "for the life of the king, and of his sons," and before Artaxerxes enjoined upon Nehemiah to teach the ignorant the laws of God in that land. The prophetic portions were probably written soon after the invasion by Sennacherib, which caused a tumult in the city, also the prayer of Hezekiah in the temple, and the avenging of Jehovah upon the Assyrians suggested in 66 : 6 ; 37 : 1–35. It surely could not have been written when the temple lay in ruins. Nor could the remonstrances against idols have been written after they had been destroyed in Babylon, and had long ceased in Judæa. Making it history creates insuperable difficulties, which disappear when regarded as prophecy. To put the writing of it soon after 700 b.c. makes it a wonderful composition of an inspired prophet, while to place it about 485 or 445 b.c. makes it a marvellous rhapsody, without coherence or possible explanation, of which no theory of a "conditional element" pervading it is an approximate solution.

To say that the passages describing a suffering Messiah and the Messiah regnant and triumphant were fulfilled before 444 b.c. is hardly paying "a decent respect to the opinions of mankind." If the writer were not Isaiah of Jerusalem, he must have flourished in the latter part of that era, being a junior companion prophet, and, like him, possessing all kinds of talent and all beauties of discourse, treating of Redemption Promised, of Redemptive Accompaniments, and of Redemption in its realization.

Very early all that now forms the Book of Isaiah was closely connected in MS. It was enrolled as canonical before the close of the prophetic era, which proves as sure as dawn precedes the day its ancient authentication. Divine Inspiration is evident all through the Book, and elucidates its contents—the vision in chapter 6 and 66 : 6. The Divine voice attests the later as well as the earlier chapters, and the later as well as the earliest Biblical Books. It chose Abraham rather than any other Semite ; it chose Isaac rather than Ishmael, Jacob rather than Esau, and the tribe of Judah as the line whence the Messiah should descend, rather than Jacob's first-born. And so Inspired Prophecy and Miraculous Events were required for the grand accomplishment of those ancient choosings. The subject really *is not* Israel, nor Cyrus, not Exile, or return from it, but *Preparation for the Redemption of the world;* Hebrew election and Gentile calling, temple sacrifices and prophetic deliverances being necessary elements in the great preparation of two thousand years. See this wrought out in " Bible Growth and Religion."

My plan did not include a notice of those writers who differ from me, which confuses the ordinary reader, and is not needed by the learned. Yet I must mention Canon Driver, who in his " Life and Times of Isaiah," as I understand him, holds that those grand chapters, 40–66, relate to One who was a Deliverer of Israel *from captivity*, and would not allow the *Babylonians* to restrain them from returning to Palestine. They shall return in grand processions, and Zion shall be rebuilt! But is not that rather small work for which to invoke Him who inhabiteth Eternity, calling to the Isles and the nations afar off to behold His wonders? Erelong those Babylonians ceased to be a nation, and the Persians possessed their lands. Never could the isles of the Mediterranean Sea nor the distant nations hear the prophet east of the Euphrates! Even when scattered through the empire before Babylon fell, no large assembly of Hebrews could be gathered into one place where the prophet might address them; and it were useless for him to lift up his voice or cry unto widely scattered captives! Of course, the prophecy is in poetic style, but its language has the ordinary meaning. Applied to residents in the cities of Judæa before the Exile, it is easily understood; but to assign it to a time when Judah was scattered over the empire obscures the sense. The learned canon overlooks this.

Nor does he explain chapter 53 according to the demands of the text. It confessedly is not applicable to any one, except the rejected and crucified Christ. For Jehovah did not lay our iniquity on Cyrus; nor was he oppressed and dumb under it, like a sheep in the hands of her shearers. He was not taken away by oppression and an unjust judgment, nor cut off prematurely, nor stricken for Israel. Not for Cyrus did they make a grave with the wicked, and with the rich in his death. Nor did the LORD bruise him and put him to grief; nor was he ever made a sin-offering for the people. The whole chapter is singularly inapplicable to Cyrus. Read it in the Revised Version.

Of Isaiah 61, St. Luke tells us that our Lord applied the first verses to Himself, thus: "To-day hath this Scripture been fulfilled in your ears" (St. Luke 4 : 16–23, Revised Version). The authority is supreme and absolute, that it could not have been fulfilled in the time of Cyrus. Our Lord forecloses all doubt as to its meaning and application. I presume Canon Driver will acknowledge its force and obligation.

III.

THE SCIENTIFIC METHOD APPLIED TO THE BIBLE.

It is only in illustration of our subject to say that we regard the foregoing pages as the outcome of the findings, if not in strict logical sequence of following the scientific method in such themes. For science has been well defined to be the knowledge of the laws which govern phenomena. It is not the law nor the phenomena, but the knowledge of those laws which govern the manifestations of nature. Hence science is knowledge, and not agnosticism. It is what men have learned and know touching this or the other matter. Hence it is the product of experience and of experiment. Such science we may apply to Revelation and to Biblical exegesis, the Bible being received upon the testimony of disinterested and truthful men. Bible religion began anew with Abraham, who had no motive to deceive his child.

1. All true history is the record of what others or we ourselves have done; the transcript of human phenomena and achievements; the knowledge of

what has been or is being done. Some one has thought, has spoken, has put the word into deed; and the record and sequence of that is science in history, in the Bible, in religion. It is not a jumble nor an aggregate, but sequence in nature, in man, in the revelations and unfoldings of Deity.

There is no such thing as science *in* nature, for nature does not know, it simply is. But our knowledge of the laws and manifestations of nature is scientific. Natural science is our knowledge of the laws which govern nature, or its manifestations. But science cannot affirm or deny the alleged dream of Alexander at Dium, nor the crossing of the Rubicon by Cæsar, nor the signing of the Declaration of Independence by our fathers. Still our knowledge of history may suggest similar occurrences; as that of the Barons of England obtaining Magna Charta from King John, the invasion of Italy by Hannibal, and the dream of Philip of Macedon. Thus our knowledge enables us to probe and test the evidence upon which a certain dream rests, or a plunge was made, or a treaty was signed.

2. With *a priori*, or *a posteriori* probabilities our science has little to do, except so far as our knowledge is concerned. Thus $2 \times 2 = 4$ is perhaps eternally true, and never will be 3 or 5. Also that water below 32° freezes on our planet. Observation and testimony certify to this, and history tells us it has been so since the beginning of human records or of geologic time. Our *a priori* notions

are corrected by experiences. Men and women of the same temperament and characteristics are not always the most happy in wedlock. The greatest of our race have left rather feeble successors: Pericles, Alexander, Cæsar, Cicero, Shakespeare, Milton, Goethe, Cromwell, Washington, Napoleon, Gibbon, Hume, Johnson, Carlyle, etc. Even in Bible story, Moses, Joshua, Samuel, and other prophets, John Baptist, St. John and St. Paul, left no heirs of mark or distinguished merit. Nor will our expectations be realized if we look for the finest potatoes, the choicest cabbages, and the fairest flowers from seeds of the largest and most perfect of their several kinds. Here experience—*i.e.*, science tells us that by the *law of reversion* the very finest seeds usually produce the poorest crops in return. Nature exhausts herself, and so teaches us to correct our otherwise reasonable expectations. The farmer and gardener learn from their elders.

So of natural science: Kepler's law of the planetary distances, Newton's law of the force of attraction, with sundry calculation tables, come to our knowledge and to the mass of mankind upon the testimony of others. We know them only at second hand. Learned professors and their humblest scholars depend upon lists and classifications which others had made for them. They have not proved them. Libraries of large volumes may be filled with the names of plants, insects, birds, fishes, mammals, including man; of geological strata and their contents, which no late scientist has proved for himself or knows of except upon the testimony of others. There are myriads of books in the various departments of knowledge which one has not examined, who accepts their results upon trust, that miracle of human confidence. Even the reports of recent observers and explorers in the flora and fauna of our world are read by few. Agnostics should be indeed modest, for they know but little, and take most of that little upon trust in the truth of what is told them. The Christian goes perhaps a step farther, but carefully sifts all testimony touching the facts of revelation and the so-called doctrines of religion. And why not? Is not the testimony to the truth of Holy Scripture as credible and trustworthy as that of Cuvier or Lyell, of Audubon or Linnæus, of Darwin or Dawson? In the world of nature, as of revelation, man ever depends upon the testimony of man. So it is time to have done with lauding the certainties of science above the so-called guesses of Revelation. Both rest on testimony. And the testimony of Christians is no more fanatical than that of scientists. Anaxagoras and Aristotle were as fanatical as St. James and St. Mark.

3. However poor a handling the clergy make of certain questions related to theology, their training for centuries was such as to fit them to be the leaders and formers of society, of the literature and of the higher life of the nations. Not only did they tame savage men into reason and culture, they also

converted and transformed them; they multiplied copies of the ancient writings and of Holy Scripture, and with the dawn of modern life they supplied the people with an open Bible in Germany, England, France, and later on the world over. Wickliffe, Tyndale, and other translators and revisers of the Bible formed the language of England and America.

Indeed, the Church's methods in her search after truth have long been the same as those pursued in our State courts, but without a party concerned to suppress important facts. Our theological seminaries worthy of the name seek for the facts and origins of their ecclesiastical and dogmatic systems. Unlike colleges which teach Greek, Roman, and other ancient literatures as they find them in current texts, the theologian is taught and required to sift his text and the authority for it, as well as its interpretation. This did Lightfoot, Westcott, Ellicott, Cheyne, etc., in England; Turner, Briggs, Green, Harper in America; and numbers whom every scholar knows on the European continent. They seek for the right text to interpret as well as for the right principles of interpretation.

But judging from recent utterances on both sides the ocean, one might suppose that the Christian Church had *not* ever been the teacher of good ethics, culture, and criticism; that she had not led in the ways of learning and of civilization. She founded the colleges of the old world, and also many of our land—Harvard, Yale, Columbia, with many of recent date, whose chairs she has filled with Christian scholars. From Bede to Abelard and the two Bacons, Roger and Sir Francis, the path is strewn with the works of Christian writers—of Cædmon and Lanfranc, Anselm and Chaucer, Gower, Froissart and Mandeville, Sir T. More and William Tyndale. Even Spenser, Shakespeare, and Rare Ben Jonson received inspiration from the literature of the Church. She gave lawyers to the State and judges to the bench ; she humbled Henry IV., of Germany, and Frederick, the Redbeard ; she softened the asperity of barons, incited to chivalry and the Crusades, conquered the barbarians who trampled down the old civilization ; and when Constantinople fell to the Turks she received and provided for her exiled scholars. The New World was peopled by her colonists, who copied her attainments in life and in arts, as well as in science and religion. But she does not so often talk about what she has done as of what remains to be done.

Thus she illustrates what Bishop Thompson tersely says in his Lectures : " The beast eats the phenomena, or drinks it, and thinks no more about it." So she follows the scientific way of seeking truth, she absorbs it, inculcates it upon others, but says little about it. Even of the Sermon on the Mount she inquires what and where it is before she expounds it. So of this or that miracle, at the Red Sea, at Gadara, at Olivet, she first certifies to the record, and then accepts and teaches it. Now one of her sons devotes his studies to the prophets, now to the Gospels, now to the Epistles, and now to the primitive records of mankind and the early Christians.

4. Whether St. Paul's writings stimulate and exalt the religious sense is not enough for the Church to know, but she is bound to know, from reasonable evidence of their date, style, character, and early acceptance, that they are the writings of St. Paul. That is the scientific method. So of the Epistles of St. Peter and St. John and of the Fourth Gospel.

There are confessedly some old Apocryphal writings which are true as history, true and elevating in ethic, but which are not accounted by the Church universal as inspired ; for they never received prophetic endorsement and attestation. Hence, despite their quality, they are not included in the canon of Holy Scripture.

We all remember the recent work of the revisers of the Old and New Testament ; that some fourscore scholars were long engaged in deciding upon their text and its proper translation into modern English ; and that in several instances they eliminated portions of the text ; for example, St. John 8 : 1–11 ; 1 Ep. St. John 5 : 7–9 ; the Doxology to the Lord's Prayer following St. Matt. 6 : 13, with other lesser changes. These we may examine for ourselves and judge of the method and its result, while we assume no superior learning. A text has been furnished which for the most part is up to modern scholarship, and bears the test of Greek criticism.

For the reasons that the Church allows such emendation of canonical Scripture, she rejects the story of Augustine, that the flesh of the peacock never decays, for which Mr. Burroughs laughs at the saint. But to hold the Church responsible for it is extremely unjust.

Since the Council of Nicæa, the assembled Church has never promulgated a mere opinion as a doctrine of salvation, or necessary to be believed. Rather has she inquired in the true scientific way, What was taught in the beginning? How did the early teachers and bishops understand the question? What is the teaching of Scripture about it? Neither primitive Christianity nor the Orthodox Christianity of to-day requires men to believe in the *development of doctrines of salvation*. These were revised and authenticated by our Lord and His Apostles, and they may not be added to or diminished. Questions of polity and of discipline may be changed or modified to suit the times, but the whole Church assembled in Council has no power to change doctrines of salvation.

So St. Paul, in Gal. 1 : 8, " Though we, or an angel from heaven, should preach unto you any gospel other than that which we have preached unto you, let him be anathema ;" and he repeats the curse for so doing in the next verse. The doctrines of salvation were given at the first ; the Church and her heralds are but the teachers of the Glad Tidings, which never change. No law of reversion pertains to Christ, but He enjoins His people to go on unto perfection in the Faith once delivered to them. Ours it is to ask what was first taught ; how that teaching has been preserved ; and whether we now have trustworthy records of it ? We may reject all later additions and insertions to the Creed of Christ and the primitive Church. Such is the scientific method applied to theology and to Christian history. It is the law of religious phenomena whereby we may weigh the spiritual manifestations.

5. And when we consider intellectual processes and achievements, what becomes of our science ? We find in Macbeth and in the Comus what no previous writer of our tongue had led us to expect, a sort of literary miracle. There is a touch and a fancy quite unexpected, something which our soul appropriates as well as our mind. It is immortal as mind. It is not merely the words we read, but their deeper meaning disclosed by their setting. Yet there was nothing in the times and the unfoldings which environed Shakespeare and Milton that would naturally produce such work. In other words, their work was not expected before they exemplified their talents. And so it has been with all great achievements of the mind. The material wonders of Morse and Edison were only guessed as possible after the experiments of Franklin and New-

ton and Francis and Roger Bacon. Chemistry and physics are prophetic of mysterious phenomena, and miracle is merged in expectation. In the material world the unexpected rarely happens. We have forecasts of the weather, and of this or that discovery. But none of these discoverers of telephones and continents can sing like the Bard of Avon and of Paradise Lost.

So in the Sermon on the Mount there is purity unexcelled and nobility of sentiment unsurpassed, which uttered in that age and in that "outlandish corner of Judæa" are even more wonderful than the originality. And if we consider it a Divine prophecy of the ethics which shall yet prevail on this earth, that surely makes its utterance then all the more wonderful. To be smitten on the one cheek and then offer the other to the smiter is a prophecy of conduct which concerns the smiter as well as the smitten. For it suggests a principle of action becoming operative among men, when the rude hand of a smiter shall be as rare a surprise as it now is for the smitten one to turn the other cheek. It is there, more than in the purity and nobility of the sentiment, that the Divineness lies and the superiority of the Speaker consists. He, with all the human odds and environment against Him, then uttered a code of ethics which He foresaw would become the heritage and the rule of mankind. Milton, in the "Comus," was only a copyist of that prophecy. To the sister is ascribed that deep-souled purity, that true unsuspicion of evil, which makes her strong against a thousand dangers. Of the power of magic she had no experience and no fears, but her more knowing brothers were all the more anxious for her rescue. They feared to trust perfect, but inexperienced innocence with a consummate trickster, whose strength might win the mastery. And the rule is safe for all untried characters.

But we are told of One who did resist a consummate master in all wicked arts, and it was before He spoke that famous Sermon. Why shall we accept His discourses, yet discredit His encounters and achievements? What quality is there in the utterance which was not in the Person? Why shall we immortalize His words while we refuse immortality to Him and to His Person? But it is becoming the fashion to deny the raising of Lazarus and the resurrection of our Lord, though His words of comfort to the sisters are admitted to be genuine and His later words to His disciples! There they were to end except in memory! The Soul that bore them, the minds of the greatest among men—Moses, Samuel, Elijah, Paul, Plato, Pascal—despite of all their celestial qualities, are to end like the grass or like the grain eaten by a beast! And soul-powers which are perfect in their manifestations to the last moment of mortal life shall cease like the herbage of the field when cut down on a sunny day, and their life go out with the sunset!

And this because of our ignorance, and that we have had no experience of continued life other than in our posterity, or in posthumous reputation!

6. We saw how the mental achievements were unexpected till accomplished by those whom we have named; we have seen and known how much in life is taken upon trust, and that in the world of matter its analysis, nomenclature, classifications, are also taken upon trust in what others have done in their several lines of work, and that systems and sciences are built upon them from Copernicus to Kepler, Newton, Darwin, and Spencer; why then may we not proceed in similar lines of discovery in the realm of mind and soul and God? Why shall we stumble at "Thy brother shall rise again," "Whosoever believeth in Me shall never die!" since upon the uniform testimony of all who knew Him—five hundred at one time—He who spoke those new words did actually Himself rise again? Every recurrence of Easter, every Lord's day, certifies to it as surely as that the Passover testifies to the Exodus! The Hebrew had his Passover and the restoration of the son of the widow of Zarephath; but the Christian has the daughter of Jairus, the widow's son at Nain, Brother Lazarus, JESUS in His Resurrection and Ascension, all testifying to the power and truth of Him who restored life.

As we receive the records of the Old Testament and of the New upon testimony which has been thoroughly probed, we follow the scientific method as closely as any scientist who accepts the findings and classifications of others; indeed, more so, for the Church has borne constant witness to what she received, while the investigations of scientists have been but occasional and sporadic. They have no perpetual witness like that of Hebrew and Christian writers. So even the Resurrection was not a *new* experience. The new thing about it was that one should come to life and rise from the grave without the intervention of known personal agency. Other revivifications were by recognized prophets like Elijah, Elisha, and by Him who, after raising others, was Himself raised from the grave. Indeed, St. Matthew says that the Pharisees *expected* this, and by the order of Pilate went and made the sepulchre sure, sealing the stone to make it safe, the guard being with them (27 : 63–66). And the earliest Christian art, as well as preaching, agrees in the representation. The resurrection of JESUS CHRIST was expected, and had been foretold. The only question for us is, are the accounts true?

Hence, we also ask, are the accounts true that Columbus discovered any part of America and that Sir Walter Raleigh found potatoes and tobacco here, which were new to Europeans? Or shall we take those accounts like the humorous story of Charles Lamb of how the Chinese first learned of roast pig? He, however, does not deny the previous existence of pigs. Nor did Raleigh deny the existence of potatoes and tobacco. But they were a new experience with him. Yet a "scientist" lately dogmatizes that, "What we know, we know *only* through the senses!" How, then, can we know who discovered America? or whether Europeans first learned of potatoes and tobacco from the American Indians? or whether Cæsar ever conquered Britain? or whether the Declaration of Independence was written by those who are said to have written it? How does the scientist know the true from the spurious? whether his coffee is genuine or adulterated? whether his sugar is from cane or corn? his paper made of cotton or linen, and his cloth dyed with Indigo or Prussian blue? Scientists, like Christians, take much of their knowledge at second hand. Both largely depend upon the testimony of others. If one can demonstrate a fact, the other feels the witness to what he believes abiding within him (1 Ep. St. John 3 and 4).

7. Yet he is *not* all heart and feeling and subjectivity. He believes in objective truths, doctrines, and revelations which were duly certified to in old times by Abraham, Moses, Samuel, Isaiah, Ezra, by our Lord and His Apostles. The testimony has received continuous certifications in its passage through the centuries. This is but the alphabet of our religion. All theologians of repute maintain the necessity of belief in the objective revelation of God as well as in subjective faith in Christ; in religious truth as well as religious feeling. And so the

witness in the soul of a devout man testifies to the power of a great Saviour. Behold the martyrs!

Thus, he who decries the scientific method in Christians exemplifies his ignorance of Christian training in the principles of investigation. We deprecate all mere assumption and the blind following of a theory. We require proof of all we believe. We are taught to " read, mark, learn, and inwardly digest ;" to be ever ready to give to the inquirer a reason for our belief ; to prepare in time for the joys and unfoldings of eternity. We are to *know Him* in whom we believe ; to worship an objective God by means of an objective agency such as we find in the Church.

If it be said that the Church has no *original* copy of the Holy Scriptures, it must not be forgotten that she was the *living witness* to their authenticity when first given ; so that for the Scriptures of the time of David we have her living testimony in that age, so of the time of Hezekiah, of Jeremiah, and of Ezra ; men of learning quite competent to do so passed upon the Scriptures of that time ; they had the living testimony of those who received the written Word, and God bore them witness.

Then of the Septuagint at the close of the third century B.C., the witnessing Church certified to the Sacred Writings and accepted a translation which to-day asserts itself, and is becoming more and more recognized as of equal authority with the Hebrew text. Schrader claims that the more exact

7*

forms of Hebrew words and names are those preserved in the Septuagint ; and he cites the Assyrian Bin-hidri—*i.e.*, Ben-hadra, in illustration. (Schaff's Herzog, *sub* Benhadad.)

When we study the era of Origen and of Jerome, what is more unscientific than to say that these men in their collation and translation of Hebrew and Greek Scriptures did not have access to trustworthy copies of the ancient text? Why, the "Hexapla" of Origen proves the contrary. Athenagoras and Justin Martyr are witnesses of the fact. Indeed, Cuvier, Darwin, and Spencer collate *supposed* facts and specimens to elucidate their theories which have not a tenth part of the evidence of genuineness as have the Hebrew and Greek text which we receive to-day. There were schools of the prophets from Samuel to Jeremiah ; while from Ezra to Mattathias, and from our Lord to Jerome, the Church, Hebrew and Christian, testified to the Sacred Books. What facts of science or of history are more strongly attested ?

One-half of the three years' course in our theological seminaries is devoted to Biblical and Church history, to evidences which authenticate the genuineness and credibility of the Old and New Testament, to the rules and principles of correct interpretation. Some knowledge of the languages in which the Bible was written is required, not as an exercise in grammar and syntax, but the better to understand that Bible and how to explain it correctly. Christianity has a history as well as offices, functions, and usages ; and these are to be studied along with the Scriptures upon which it is founded. Indeed, how to reach a correct exegesis of Scripture is much longer dwelt upon than how to preach to the people. The method is scientific, even if the preaching is poor.

However, they who have never taken such a course are not the men to lecture the Church on how to apply the scientific method to exposition of the Bible. It cannot be done in a sermon of a Sunday. To explain the creation of man in Genesis by the legend of Bel's head being cut off, and the blood which flowed from his body being mixed with the earth or clay from which the first man was God-made and endowed with the Divine life, will be easier to do after the Chaldean account in Genesis is more generally known.

So of Gen. 3 : 15. The old Hindus had a saviour and serpent-killer in Krishna, one of their Avatars, who " was not altogether invulnerable, for when he crushed the head of the serpent of Jumna he was poisoned in the heel, and was cured only by drinking the milk of the goddess Parvati Durga, the Warrior, from whose eye the goddess Kalli sprang in complete armor, like Minerva from the head of Jupiter." See the collocation of " Legends of a Redeemer" in " God Enthroned in Redemption," pp. 7-37. The variations in the legends emphasize the truth of our Genesis, while the legends of early belief in God and His worship overturn Mr.

Spencer's theory of the evolution of religion among men.

In all phenomena, spiritual and material, objective or subjective, the first inquiry is for the evidence upon which the manifestations depend. As in the case of the demoniac of Gadara, we are told who was the Healer, what was the disease, and the subject of it. We have Christ, an evil spirit, and the man possessed. It is no more wonderful than other instances of healing, except that an evil power or entity had been permitted to enter and possess a man. Is this any more marvellous than the evil power, called the serpent, which entered Eden and tempted Mother Eve? Admit the first recorded instance of Satanic influence, and all that follow are quite explicable. What became of the expelled demon is of no account. He was not destroyed, but only expelled; and not being disabled, he went and took possession of another, or rather the legion possessed another company of creatures. The history of the occurrence, if it stand the test of being a truthful record, must be received just as we accept any other narrative, as, for example, the history of the martyrs. And every martyrdom for Jesus Christ attests His life and works, as well as the faith of the martyred and the doctrines of Christianity. There is a joint testimony of the objective and subjective.

But because we to-day have no experience of such healing and such martyrdom we ought not to call it unscientific to believe they ever occurred ; for they were just as real at the time as the inscriptions on Egyptian tombs and the tablets of Babylonia, which were long buried out of sight. The testimony of primitive man and of contemporary history may be as credible as what we see about us. And there are universal beliefs, concepts, records, legends which, because they are so universal, must be regarded as true. Among these is belief in evil spirits in Eden, in Babylon, in Egypt and Iran. Every ancient people had a devil of some sort. Every ancient literature embodies the idea as a fact, and also how to cure its hurt and evade its power. The thought is no more prevalent or potent in Judæa than in Egypt, in Bactria, and in Babylonia. So it becomes as clearly the affirmation of science as anything propounded by Darwin or H. Spencer. The attestations of universal mankind must be accepted as scientific and in the highest degree credible. Indeed, a true record commands belief. See chapter 4, touching Legends of Evil Spirits in "God in Creation."

8. Recent discovery of ancient facts also confirms the fact and the time of the Sojourn in Egypt. Thus, R. S. Poole has called attention to Mr. Groff's identification of two names of prominence in the Pentateuch, in the lists of Karnak, among the tribes made prisoners at Megiddo by Thothmes III. —viz., Jacob-El and Joseph-El, transposed or shortened a little. Some Hebrews during this obscure

period were engaged in border wars and even in military service abroad. This is consonant with the story of the death of Ephraim's sons in a border foray (1 Chron. 7 : 20, 21), and the fact that the Israelites marched out of Egypt in battle array (Ex. 13 : 18). The *American Register*, of Paris, remarks of the report to the Academy of Inscriptions and Belles Lettres, after a thorough discussion of the subject, that, "It is more than likely—and in this consists the great value of this new version—that in this fact we have gained a clew to an episode in the history of the children of Israel between their arrival in Egypt and exodus."

It means that Thothmes III. in his wars in Palestine captured two persons who were worshippers of El, and were probably Hebrews. One bore the name Jacob, the other Joseph, named after those patriarchs. They were carried to Egypt by Thothmes III. in the sixteenth century B.C. Our Bible Jacob was already dead, and Thothmes may have been the "king who knew not Joseph," a successor of those who expelled the Hyksos.

The mummy of Sekenen-Ra, who had been mortally wounded in the contest, and that of Rameses II. were found in a vault near Thebes in 1881. And Rameses II. took great pains to erase the names of Hyksos and other kings from the statues at Bubastis, and to inscribe his own in their place. Miss Edwards shows that Joseph served under two kings. The first of them was Apepi, who probably killed

Sekenen-Ra. Other findings disclose that the Israelites were held in servitude after the expulsion of the shepherd kings.

M. Naville, as the result of Egyptian exploration work, in 1885 rehabilitated old Pithom, its thick walls and edifices built by the Israelites, some bricks with straw and some without straw, when the heavy hand of Rameses II. lay hard upon them. His name is the oldest of any one found in this border fort and store-city. It was his own work, and not, as at Bubastis, an usurpation, the name of Rameses II. inscribed on the work of his predecessors. Pithom, indeed, now certifies to the name of the Pharaoh and Exodus to the people who built it. Thus, the recovered works and the ancient record supplement each other. The bricks prove their builders and when they wrought.

In Schrader's "Cuneiform Inscriptions," vol. 2, p. 147, we learn that Jonah must have lived and delivered his message to the Ninevites a century before Sargon II. built Khorsabad. Under him Nineveh embraced Kalah, Rehoboth, and Dûr-Sarrukin. Including these towns, the circumference of the capital would be about ninety miles, or more than three days' journey for a footman, more nearly five days' journey. So the population, including 120,000 that could not discern between right and wrong, or under eight years of age, is not overestimated in Jonah 4 : 11 ; nor its greatness of three days' journey round it in 3 : 3, 4. Our scientific method confirms the text. We find illustrations in Egypt, Assyria, Babylon, and India of the historical and prophetical portions of Scripture.

We have to deal with matters far more tangible than sentiment, feelings, and emotions; we have dogmatic formulas, historical records, and a God-given Revelation to prove and illustrate. Consideration of comparative religion is quite young, but it must receive attention, and so of different forms of Christianity. What is the effect of dogma in Scotland and in Italy? What is the outcome of Creed or the want of Creed in America? Where there is a blending of Creed with Conduct are the people more soundly Christian in faith and works? What is the relation between doing the will and knowing the doctrine?

9. How can we meet the statement that " the *Resurrection* is a myth which is kept alive because mankind have such a profound interest in believing it?" Thus, for example: The Resurrection is but the authentication by JESUS CHRIST of life without the body, in which men have believed ever since fossil men provided an eternal habitation for their dead, and placed amulets in the skulls of the deceased in order to secure happiness and exemption from evil in the disembodied state; in which men showed their belief by the judgment scenes of Amenti in Egypt, in the Realm of Allat, and Life Eternal in the land of the silver sky of Babylonia, and in various legends touching immortality; all

which are unfolded in "God in Creation" and in "Bible Growth and Religion." It was believed before Abraham lived or the Lord arose, before St. Paul preached it, or Athenagoras was converted to it, or Justin Martyr died for it; and it has become the accepted belief of many who had been unbelievers, from the first to the nineteenth century.

But this should not prevent a scientific searching for the facts of history and the phenomena of the Spirit of God, so that others may know why Christians to-day believe in the Resurrection of their Lord, and that His followers eighteen hundred years ago so believed. That we now have no experience of such events is really no more oppugnant to the facts than, because continents are not now discovered and Britain is not now conquered, therefore the story of Columbus and of Julius Cæsar is false! Yet doubters of old came to believe in it. As well might the Indian deny salt and sugar to be in use anywhere before Europeans brought them to his notice. As well might the East Indian prince deny the veracity of the traveller who told him that in his country the water became so hard in winter that men walked on it and so crossed over rivers! Precisely so is it with them who "know only what they know through the senses." The senses, indeed, disclose only a small part of human knowledge.

10. Moreover, may we not trust to our intuitions and soul perceptions as well as to what we know through our sense perceptions? So that when we

have done with glaciers and moths, protoplasm and materialistic studies, with all other human culture, learning and proving all that we can ever learn and prove, we may have the assurance not only of rest, but of blessedness. For seeds die to live again in plant and flower; from dying life to springing life is the law of the things we see about us. Nature does not disappoint proper expectations. She is no more cruel than she is kind : she is Nature.

Why, then, shall the minds she has matured and ripened, the souls she has filled with thoughts of God and longings for immortality, have no continuance in that environment where they can best unfold their possibilities? More surely than the boyhood of Shakespeare and Milton prophesied of their future achievements does the spirit of a thoughtful man prophesy of the opportunities which shall hereafter be afforded him.

Neither the be-all nor the end-all is here and now for any man of aspiration and soul growing qualities. If in his studies of things and of life, of suns and stars, he also studies soul life and spiritual being, he will come to know what soul life is, and that there is for him a never-ending life with One who Himself rose from the dead. *Because* He lives, shall all who believe in Him live also. But how can these things be? Yes, how can you color an apple or perfume a rose? Why is your child's eye blue when your own is brown? Why is ice formed in winter and the sheep shorn every spring? Because it is according to the law of their being. So it is according to the law of being a Christian that he shall live forevermore with the Lord who ransomed him from death. He is the Resurrection and the life for all believers. His ways are from everlasting to everlasting. All who hunger and thirst for immortality shall find it in Him. His was an *opened* grave! There was a vision of Angels! They were seen in Eden; they were seen by Abraham and Jacob; they appeared in the Garden, and again at Olivet. Is not that sufficient attestation? Doubt not His power. It is the law of spiritual phenomena. Spiritual life is dependent upon the Giver of it. Because He lives, you shall live also.

Thus have we sought to illustrate how the scientific method may be applied to the study of the Bible, to the doctrines of salvation, and the desire for immortality. Said Victor Hugo: " Winter is on my head and eternal spring is within my heart. The violets and the roses are beautiful as ever. The fragrance finds capacity of enjoyment. The grave is but a thoroughfare; it closes with the sunset and opens with the dawn.'' Says another poet:

> " Every noblest aspiration
> Is God's angel, undefiled,
> And in every 'O my Father!'
> Slumbers deep a ' Here, my child!' "

Thus there is an eternal tendency in men to desire and pray for admittance to that abode where life "immortal blooms."

To see that I have not overstated the assumptions and dependence of science, the reader may compare Professor J. T. Huxley on "The Advance of Science the last Half Century." On page 34 he says, "Any one who is practically acquainted with scientific work is aware that those who refuse to go beyond fact rarely get as far as fact; and any one who has studied the history of science knows that almost every great step therein has been made by the 'anticipation of nature'—that is, by the invention of hypotheses which, though verifiable, often had very little foundation to start with, and turned out wholly erroneous in the long run."

Mr. Huxley illustrates this by the guesses of astronomy, of which Kepler's was the wildest; by several hypotheses of Newton's; for observation cannot go beyond the limit of our faculties; while even within those limits we cannot be certain that any observation is absolutely exact and exhaustive. And our observation at one time may prove untrue when our powers, directly or indirectly, are enlarged.

Kepler's assumption that the planets moved in ellipses was only an approximate truth; for as a fact, the centre of gravity of a planet describes neither an ellipse nor any other simple curve, but an immensely complicated undulating line. It may be doubted whether any generalization based upon physical data is absolutely true. The *invention* of verifiable hypotheses is not only permissible, but is one of the conditions of progress (pp. 35-38), for Mr. Huxley knows through the senses, and through guesses and assumptions ! Beyond that even metaphysical theology does not venture.

In the ideas and definitions of matter, atomic, molecular, cosmic ; of force and motion, he shows it is questionable whether science to-day has much advanced beyond that of Aristotle twenty-three centuries ago. We may describe our 65 to 68 recognized "elements," but whether they all run into atoms or ether, into molecules or gases cannot be determined ! The name "New Chemistry" is very significant (pp. 40–62). We have also "New Astronomy" and "New Physics" after five thousand years' study and observation !

Modern protoplasm does not prove the assumption of "spontaneous generation ;" for it "has utterly broken down in every case which has been properly tested. Yet belief in it was accepted by all philosophers down to the latter part of the seventeenth century, when Redi shook it to its foundations ; Schwann and others proved it to be untrustworthy just fifty years ago" (pp. 118, 119).

Thus this corypheus of modern science guesses and assumes as true a thousandfold more than a dozen orthodox expositors of the Bible. He and they alike depend upon testimony.

But while Professor Huxley denies the claims of Mr. Burroughs, he, in a recent *Nineteenth Century*, shows himself as reckless of historic testimony as he is daring in assumptions for science. He fails to see that whether the Canon of St. Paul's in 1890 agrees with the Canon of St. Paul's thirty years before it does not affect the now historical fact of the literary attainments of Babylonians and Egyptians 2500 to 3000 years B.C., nor of the Bible patriarchs 2000 to 1500 B.C. So, his scorn of ancient legends in Babylon and Egypt will not avail to minimize the "stories" of Genesis. For they are as well founded as his guesses of science.

If $2 + 2 + 4 = 8$ in science, why do they not equal the same in history? Our religion rests upon the testimony of patriarchs and prophets and national records during two thousand years, and of at least one million other Hebrews during fifteen hundred years; of JESUS and His apostles and the first century Christians. Now, if we may not believe their testimony as handed down through those ages, neither may we believe any allegation of science or of secular history during those ages, nor anything which Professor Huxley alleges of the ancient philosophers; for their testimony is no more credible than that of Hebrew and Christian religionists.

Since his "Half Century" essay in 1887 we are quite prepared for any historical assumptions or denials in another essay in the middle of 1890. He appears not to know that the demonstrations of history require us to accept as true as any science the records of Babylonia and Egypt in the third millennium B.C., and of the Bible patriarchs in the second millennium B.C. And he probably discerns the sophistry of his own attempt to make the Bible responsible for the miscalculations of biblical chronologists ! It nowhere says, Now the Flood occurred 1600 years after the creation of the World !

The Independent of August 28th, 1890, prints a letter from Prof. A. H. Sayce, a short extract from which must end this chapter :

"The discoveries made by Mr. Petrie prove that in Palestine, as in Egypt and Assyria, there are monuments of the past hidden beneath the soil which go back not only to the age of the Kings, but even to that older Canaanitish period which preceded the invasion of the Israelites. Among the cuneiform tablets found at Tel el-Amarna, in Egypt, are dispatches from the Governor of Lachish to the Egyptian monarch. The dispatches imply that there was an Archive-chamber in which their duplicates and the answers to them were preserved. It is more than possible that the Archive-chamber with its precious contents may still be lying within the walls discovered by Mr. Petrie, awaiting only a few more weeks of digging to be brought to light. Inscriptions and sculptured monuments will yet be found to pour floods of unexpected light upon the records of the Old Testament."

IV.

ANCIENT BABYLONIANS AND EGYPTIANS NOT TOTEMISTS.

As in recent public lectures upon Egypt the speaker asked whether totemism did not early exist in the land of the hawk and the crocodile, which were symbols of their gods, I offer a few facts which may suggest that such could not be so in primitive times. Yet very early in history misconceptions of the story of the serpent in Eden travelled far and wide, and led to its adoration. It symbolized the Deity. Still, in Babylonia, in Egypt, and under the Theocracy of the Hebrews there ever existed two important facts of a character opposed to totemism: First, the monarchy; and second, the intermarriage of kindred and members of the same tribe or clan. Egyptians even killed their supposed totems, which are often confounded with religious symbols. These facts are opposed to totemism. Kings, from the mythical Osiris to Thothmes II., in the sixteenth century B.C., and much later, married their sisters. It was a common practice among the Pharaohs. So in old Chaldea Abraham married

NOT TOTEMISTS. 169

his half-sister, which serves to illustrate the custom there at that time ; while Isaac and Jacob married their cousins. This practice does not coexist with totemism, which forbids such marriages. (See "Encyclopædia Britannica," art. Totemism.)

Nor does monarchy coexist with totemism. Yet from the earliest times, from Osiris to Menes and Sneferu, kings reigned in Egypt ; while from Nimrod to Khammuragas and Sargon I. kings reigned in Babylonia. Among the early Hebrews God was their King. This continued from Abraham to Saul and David.

Again, before historic times, the myths tell us of Horus, who speared the crocodile, one of the supposed early totems of Egypt, and her sculptures graphically portray him in the act of spearing a serpent. Babylonian legends describe Bel-Merodach as fighting against the old dragon-totem of that country, and the cylinders vividly represent the fierce combat. Iranian Bactria had her Sosiosh, who turned evil into good, who slew serpents and scorpions, and wrought redemption for her people ; while the Indian Krishna killed the huge serpent of Jumna. See chapter 1 of "God Enthroned in Redemption."

Thus, from the nature of the case and the oppugnancy between rival powers, totemism could not coexist with monarchy nor with intermarriage between kinsmen and clansmen. If the totem were anything more than a symbol or ensign, it could

8

not be tolerated within a monarchy, for the king was superior to all other earthly powers. His superior was the celestial Being known as God-Amun, God Osiris, God-Ra, God-Il, or God-Merodach, whose worship excluded all place and scope for deified totems. And the custom of intermarriage between the tribes and clans of a kingdom largely negatived and precluded the possible union of rival gods. The totemism found among our Indians and others in modern times is far too late to illustrate the worship of totems in ancient Babylonia and in Egypt.

It is interesting to note that Thothmes III., of the first half of the sixteenth century B.C., was the maker of the obelisk which is now in our Central Park. He was a famous Pharaoh of one of the best defined periods of Egyptian history. Yet, singularly enough, Mr. H. Spencer cites him to illustrate his theory of ancestor-worship, and connects him quite closely with the builder of the Great Pyramid, which was a thousand years before him, even according to the shorter chronology—*i.e.*, of the fourth dynasty.

The Egyptian poet-laureate makes the god Ammon to address Thothmes III. as " the blazing sun, shining like a god before the enemy ; as a young bull which none can approach ; as a crocodile, terrible in the waters, not to be encountered ; as a lion, fierce of eye, who leaves his den and stalks through the valley ; as the hovering hawk which seizes whatever pleases him ; and as the jackal of the South, who prowls through the land." Mr. Spencer adds the epithet of an older translation, calling him " the valiant bull Horus, reigning over the Thebaid."

I fail to discover ancestor worship or any form of totemism in these appellatives. Thothmes has here *seven* different characters attributed to him, and is addressed by the names of five supposed totems ; also as the Sun and as Horus ; the last two having well-defined positions and origins. It is a comparison which contains its own refutation.

Moreover, Hatasu, the sister of Thothmes III., calls herself " the living Horus, abounding in divine gifts, the mistress of diadems, rich in years (she was then under forty), the golden Horus, Queen of Upper and Lower Egypt, daughter of the Sun (her father was Thothmes I.), consort of Ammon (she had married her own brother, Thothmes II.). She also called herself " the daughter of Ammon, dwelling in his heart, and living forever !" The self-adulation is too apparent for remark.

The royal brother and sister use some of the *same titles* indifferently. They are each Horus, the living Horus, or the golden Horus, or the valiant bull Horus. They are the son of a god, and the daughter of a god, though their parents (Thothmes I. and his consort) were well known. Not worshippers of their ancestors, they most extravagantly extol themselves by means of their acknowledged deity. The

"Queen of diadems and daughter of the Sun" was the sister of him who is styled "crocodile, hawk, bull, lion, jackal," all by the same rhapsodist. Not a word of prayer is uttered, nor sacrifice offered, only self-glorification, in Oriental exuberance, is expressed. Truly, may we not say that the builder of our New York obelisk and his sister Hatasu are sufficient answers to totemism in ancient Egypt?

While they adored the Sun-god and worshipped Ammon, they assuredly did not worship their progenitors. Moreover, the earliest Egyptian kings speared the totem-crocodile, and the earliest Babylonian kings hunted the lion, while the monarchs of both regions pursued other beasts of prey and attributed to themselves the striking characteristics of those animals. So we say "Richard of the Lion's Heart," the "Black" Prince, "Rough and Ready," "Stonewall" Jackson, etc. The reader will find much condensed information touching ancient religions in "God Enthroned in Redemption" and in "Bible Growth and Religion." "Records of the Past" and Brugsch's "Egypt" give the laudation of Thothmes III.

Moreover, the Sabeans of Arabia, the rise of whose kingdom Hommel puts at about 900 B.C., worshipped the sun, and also Sin, the moon-god, as well as Istar or Astarte. One of the tribes worshipped the sun under the form of an eagle, another under the form of a horse, and a third tribe under the form of a lion. This was a thousand years after

Abraham, and discloses the development of religious worship in a direction very different from that claimed by totemists and evolutionists. But we are told that " Jewish influence made itself felt in the future birthplace of Mahomet, and introduced those ideas and beliefs which subsequently had so profound an effect upon the birth of Islam " (*Old and New Testament Student* for March, 1890). Yet that was not till Christianity had long influenced Jewism. The actual course was from the religion of Abraham to that of ninth century B.C. totemism, thence to Jewism as influenced by Christianity at the rise of the prophet of Arabia, in 622 A.D.

Professor W. Robertson Smith, in his " Religion of the Semites," may deceive himself and his readers into supposing that the Arabians are fair illustrations of a theory of totemism and the evolution of a monotheistic religion. But he is much too late and fanciful in his citations. For we have evidence that two or three thousand years before his Arabians appeared in that country, Babylonians on the one side, and Egyptians on the other, took possession of it, quarried its mines and its hills, inscribed their names on the rocks of the Wady Magharah, and that Egyptian soldiers worked the turquoise mines of Sinai for the benefit of Sneferu or Soris, the first of the fourth dynasty. It is much too late to turn askance from the evidences of a civilization on the Nile and the Euphrates in the third, and even fourth millennium B.C. It is, therefore, a prime necessity for Professor Smith, and those who agree with his notions, to explain how contact with it had no effect on the Arabians, and also to explain whence came those Arabians whom he cites as exemplars. It were indeed easy to affirm that there were no such Arabians in the earliest times, and none who had not drifted away from their northeastern or southwestern neighbors. Arabia itself was not then peopled, Abraham was not born, and his sons by Keturah had not possessed that country. The Bible account of its inhabitants makes all easy to understand; but to put a savage people there without touch of influence from Babylonians or Egyptians is the acme of assumption. (See Sayce's "Empires of the East" and Rawlinson's "Egypt.")

China, also, which was *peopled* by emigrants *from Babylonia*, in 2300 B.C., and possessed their religious cult, has degenerated in her worship. The latest writer, the Rev. George Owen, of Pekin, gives, in the *Chronicle of the London Missionary Society*, the following graphic account of the deterioration of the religion of the Chinese: "The history of China is a striking instance of the down-grade in religion. The old classics of China, going back to the time of Abraham, show a wonderful knowledge of God. There are passages in those classics about God worthy to stand side by side with kindred passages in the Old Testament. The fathers and founders of the Chinese race appear to have been monotheists. They believed in an omnipotent, omniscient, and omnipresent God, the moral Governor of the world and the impartial Judge of man.

"But gradually the grand conception of a personal God became obscured. Nature worship crept in. Heaven and earth were deified, and God was confounded with the material heavens and the powers of nature. Heaven was called father and earth mother, and became ·China's chief god. Then the sun, moon, and stars were personified and worshipped. China bowed down to 'the hosts of heaven.' The great mountains and rivers were also deified and placed among the state gods. This nature worship continues in full force to the present time. Nature has taken the place of God.

"Polytheism and idolatry followed. From the dawn of history the Chinese worshipped their ancestors, regarding the dead as in some sort tutelary deities. This naturally led to the deification and worship of deceased heroes and benefactors, till the gods of China, increasing age by age, became legion. Her well-stocked pantheon contains gods of all sorts and sizes. There are gods of heaven and earth; gods of the sun, moon, and stars; gods of the mountains, seas, and rivers; gods of fire, war, and pestilence, wealth, rank, and literature, horses, cows, and insects.

"But the degradation did not stop here. The Chinese sank lower still and became demon worshippers. Charms—long strips of paper bearing cabalistic characters in black, green and yellow—hang from the lintels of most doors to protect the house against evil spirits. Night is often made hideous and sleep impossible by the firing of crackers to frighten away the demons. Almost every village has its professional exorcist and devil-catcher. The fear of demons is the bugbear of a Chinaman's life, and much of his worship is intended to appease their wrath and propitiate their favor, and once a year, during the seventh moon, a gigantic image of the devil himself is carried in solemn procession through every town and village, followed by the populace, feasted and worshipped.

"Animal worship, too, is rife. In some parts of North China certain animals are more worshipped than the most popular gods. The fame of even the largest temples is often due not to the gods they contain, but to the supposed presence of a fairy fox, weasel, snake, hedgehog, or rat. These five animals are believed to possess the secret of immortality and the power of self-transformation, and to exercise great influence over the fortunes of men.

"I have seen crowds of men, women, and children worshipping at an ordinary fox-burrow, and I have seen one of the great gates of Pekin thronged day after day with carriages and pedestrians going to worship a fairy fox supposed to have been seen outside the city walls. Any day small yellow handbills may be seen on the walls and boardings of Pekin assuring the people that 'prayer to the venerable fairy fox is certain to be answered.'"— *Spirit of Missions for March*, 1890.

Here we have the descendants of Abraham in Arabia and of the ancient Babylonians in China testifying against modern theories of the evolution of religion. It was not from nature worship to Mosaism, which developed into Jewism, which developed into Christianity, but the other way from the revealed to the debased. Arabia and China are our witnesses.

The mistake of evolutionists of religion lies in beginning their inquiries at too late a period. Here and there may be found what looks like totemism. But it was not so in the earliest ages. For then men held a simple belief in One Being to be worshipped. Later, from misunderstanding about the Serpent of Eden, arose animal-worship and totemism.

Closely related, if not earlier, was the worship of Istar, called Nána in the Accadian texts, Istar not being found in them. The first centres of her worship were Erech and Accad. She was called "the divine Lady of Eden," "the goddess of the tree of life," "the goddess of the Vine," etc., showing that she was Eve deified. Tammuz is said to mean "the son of life," "offspring," "the only son," etc. And he was invoked as a shepherd: "O Tammuz, shepherd and lord, bridegroom of Istar, the lady of heaven, lord of Hades, lord of the shepherd's cot," etc. The poem is written in

8*

the artificial dialect which sprang up in the court of Sargon I., probably emanating from the city of Accad. So Sayce in " Hibbert Lectures" for 1887, pp. 232-66.

The many allusions to life in Eden, to the life of Abel, the descent to Hades, Abel's character as a shepherd and being invoked by shepherds, suggest that "the Lady of Eden and of the tree of life" was Mother Eve, thus early deified, and that the departed one for whom she mourned was her shepherd son Abel or Tammuz. The earliest legends of Istar and Tammuz reach back to primitive times, and seem like the very echoes of Eden. So of serpent worship. It also may be traced to the serpent of Eden.

Mr. H. Spencer draws his examples from the later periods. Thus, in his " Ecclesiastical Institutions" (pp. 692-93), he sees the difficulty that sun worship in Egypt creates for his " derivation of all beliefs from ancestor worship," and so tries to explain away sun worship and the belief that he ever had been ruler over Egypt! Whereas, the early legend of Osiris can only be thus accounted for. A page of special pleading, with a long note to convince " theologians and mythologists," will not change the fact that in Egypt sun worship preceded ancestor worship; for the sun represented the highest beneficence in nature. Osiris, as Sun-god, was before Osiris as Judge of Amenti. And kings were first deified only because they were the representatives of the Divine order, power, and goodness. Hence adoration of kings preceded adoration of ancestors. In primitive history and Old Testament exposition the date determines the environment and often expounds the text. Hymns to Amen-Ra and the Nile are of ancient date ; festal dirges belong to the eleventh dynasty ; while, according to Renouf's " Hibbert Lectures," the oldest piece of literature in the world is a " Hymn to the Maker of Heaven and Earth, Who is the Self-existent One." Compare " God in Creation," chapter 3, and chapter 1 of this book.

V.

MR. GLADSTONE ON HEBREW AND GREEK ETHICS.

(Reprinted from *The Standard* and *The Church*.)

As St. Paul rejoiced that Christ was preached, though not quite according to his method, so I rejoice that the Rock of Scripture is defended, even though imperfectly. Mr. Gladstone has succeeded in the breadth of his view and in stating points which should satisfy the reader not only as to the honesty of his plea, but that the subject is itself worthy of all his conceded ability. The homogeneity of the Old Testament, both as to matter and spirit, and its preparative character, are of the same trend throughout. It was also for the Gentile as well as for the Jew, or, as stated in a recent publication, for "Jacob and Japheth."

This book Mr. Gladstone seems not to have read, or he would not have fallen into the ethical error of his third paper, in rating the ethic of the Hebrew as lower than that of the Achaian Greeks. When he says that "the conduct of the suitors of Penelope and the actions of Paris form the worst exhibitions of human nature which come before us in the Poems" of Homer, he overlooks what so good a Grecian could not forget, that Penelope herself was a striking exception to the prevailing laxity of her day, and that Ulysses, her husband, was ill-deserving so pure a wife. He also overlooks, what he could not forget, that the actions of Paris received large endorsement from his father and family then reigning at Troy, for they received him and the runaway wife of Menelaus, and refused to surrender her when demanded.

The " rape of Helen" is a misnomer in modern phrase. She *eloped* voluntarily with her husband's guest; she became the wife of Paris, then of his brother Deiphobus, whom she afterward betrayed in order to reconcile herself to her first husband. If our law about the receiver of stolen goods being as bad as the thief is right, the conduct of the ruling family at Troy was very reprehensible, for which neither the noble heroism of Hector, nor the loyal love of Andromache, nor the tears of Priam could atone, unless accompanied by *restitution*. And when the Poet introduces Venus to rescue Paris from the death-dealing blows of Menelaus, what is that but to sanction the adulterer's crime ?

Knowing all this, Mr. Gladstone should have boldly affirmed the lower ethics of the Greeks as compared with the Hebrews. He also overlooks what he could not forget, that King Agamemnon was himself an offender against purity when he seized the beautiful captive Briseïs, who had been awarded to Achilles. That the king had returned the daughter of the priest upon her father's demand did not justify him in seizing the prize of his ablest general. And was it less than an avenging Nemesis that Agamemnon, upon returning home from the war, found his wife an adulteress with Ægysthus, and by them was murdered? A double crime had been committed, far more heinous than that of David's, who had not thought of taking life in his amour with Bathsheba. Clytemnestra was killed for her crimes by her own son! Diomed, another of Homer's heroes, returned home after the fall of Troy, but narrowly escaped with his life from his adulterous wife, Ægiale.

Not to dwell longer upon the morality of Homer's people, both men and women, what shall we say of the Homeric gods, from Jove to Venus? Was not Olympus the rendezvous of impurity? With few exceptions its celestial denizens were quite oblivious to the observance of chastity. There is not a pure boy who has *done* his first or second year in Greek and Latin, unless the course is greatly changed since I was a youth, who is not disgusted with the amours of the gods and goddesses of the Homeric Age.

On the wrangling, the deceit and lying of Homer's gods, I must refer to Professor G. H. Gilbert's last chapter of his "Poetry of Job," Chicago, 1889.

Mr. Gladstone knows that in the historic period,

in the acme of Greek culture and attainments, the great Pericles lived for years in forbidden relations with Aspasia, and before his death accepted it as a marked favor that the Athenians legitimatized his two bastard boys! Yet he turns askance from the nativity of Pharez and Ruth! Ruth, at least, was removed by ten generations from the sin of Lot, who was not of the covenant seed, and married a Canaanitess; while Pharez was the offspring of a single desperate adventure, in order to compel the performance of lawful duty! There was nothing in them at all parallel with the sin of Agamemnon and Helen, Paris and Clytemnestra, Ulysses and Ægiale, Jove and Venus!

Moreover, Mr. Gladstone cannot forget that even Plato is an offender against good ethics. He allows men a community of women, so that the children do not know their own fathers! Indeed children were to be brought up in common, without filial or parental affection. But I may not dwell on this, and should have said less but for the great reputation of the writer and the recent strong deliverances of Rev. Dr. Charles H. Parkhurst. So I commend them and those who accept their puttings to pages 71 to 81 of "Bible Growth and Religion from Abraham to Daniel."

In Egypt, in Canaan, in Philistia, the code of ethics practised by the early Hebrews was loftier and purer than that of those peoples. It was to save his wife from dishonor as well as his own life that Abraham equivocated with Pharaoh, and with Abimelech of Gerar, each of whom sought to add Sarah to his harem ! And at the time of his equivocation Abraham was but a young Jehovist. It was more than *twenty years before* he received the covenant seal of circumcision ; while it was true that Sarah was his half sister, who to-day if introduced to strangers might be called sister Sarah. Mr. Gladstone overlooks this. He also overlooks how Dinah's brothers avenged themselves upon Hamor for his treatment of her. Their chastisement of him was not the method of men who had low views of purity and honor. But centuries later the Philistines in their treatment of Samson and his bride trampled down every law of morality. Yet in his frolics and his revenges Samson personally observed the duty of good neighborhood. As the avenger of Israel upon their oppressors, he acted officially. Compare David's treatment of Saul and consult the reference above given, also pages 166 to 174.

JACOB AND JAPHETH.

Bible Growth from Abraham to Daniel, illustrated by Contemporary History. By the author of "God in Creation," etc. 12mo, cloth, $1.25.

The Churchman says:

"The underlying motive of the book seems to be an answer to Renan's Theories of Hebrew History. It certainly succeeds in dealing with the French skeptic's reasonings pretty effectually. It shows the absurdity of the assumption that Jewish religion was merely self-originated, the outcome of special Semitic tendencies. Apart from its purpose, this volume is well worth reading, for it is written in a lively style, displays a very careful study, and is full of information on Biblical topics. It is a book we should especially commend to our readers as one likely to guide and help their study of the Bible. It takes just that large and comprehensive view which is opposed to the mere study of special and isolated verses, and gives the bearing of the earlier books of the Old Testament in a very suggestive and thoughtful way."

The New York Evangelist says:

"The author of 'God in Creation' and of 'God Enthroned in Redemption,' has given us in the present work a further development of his fundamental position, which may be briefly characterized as based upon that which Squire Wendover denied—the value of the testimony of history to revelation. A thorough and searching review of the testimony establishes very completely that the God of Israel is the very God of the whole Earth. The author is familiar with the utterances of the Higher Criticism, and with the results of recent researches among the cuneiform documents of the East, and he argues very ably and convincingly against the theory of late authorship of the Pentateuch and the Book of Daniel. Good scholarship, fine critical acumen, sound judgment, a reasonable faith, characterize this book."

BY THE SAME AUTHOR:

God in Creation and in Worship. By a Clergyman. 12mo, paper, 25 cents; cloth, 50 cents.

God Enthroned in Redemption. Part Second of "God in Creation." The answer of History to modern theories of the Evolution of Christianity. 12mo, cloth, 50 cents.

Both parts in one volume. 12mo, cloth, $1.00.

THOMAS WHITTAKER,
2 AND 3 BIBLE HOUSE, NEW YORK.

DIABOLOLOGY.

THE PERSON AND KINGDOM OF SATAN.

The Bishop Paddock Lectures for 1889.

By the Rev. EDWARD H. JEWETT, D.D.; LL.D. Second Edition. 12mo, cloth, $1.50.

CONTENTS : Lecture I.—Introductory. Lecture II.—Moral Probation. Lecture III.—Satanic Personality. Lecture IV.—Parsee and Hebrew Views Compared. Lecture V.—Christ's Teaching with Regard to Evil and the Evil One. Lecture VI.—The Sixth Petition of the Lord's Prayer.

"The lectures are timely and able, and ought to have a strong influence in counteracting the pernicious and baseless modern theory that Satan is only the personification of a mere force. The author's reasoning is unanswerable; he always is fair to opponents, and he has done good and abiding service. His pages are especially rich in researches and comparisons which bring out the differences between the Hebrew and the Parsee, or other beliefs in regard to Satan and evil spirits in general. He seems to quite disprove the hypothesis that the Jews borrowed the ideas of the Persians on these subjects."
—*The Congregationalist.*

"He has carefully and critically examined the various views and teachings on this subject to bring out with great logical clearness the truth of the personality of Satan as taught in the New Testament as well as in the rest of Holy Scripture."—*The Churchman.*

"The author deserves credit for the boldness and clearness with which his investigation is conducted."—*The Virginia Sem. Magazine.*

"Although written primarily for the scholarly public, the style is simple and the language clear and easily comprehensible by the ordinary reader."—*The Philadelphia Press.*

"This volume discusses, in a thorough and scholarly manner, the question of the personality of spirits, good and evil, their probation, and the place assigned to them in the teachings of the Bible."
—*National Baptist.*

THOMAS WHITTAKER,

2 AND 3 BIBLE HOUSE, NEW YORK.

CANON ROW'S NEW BOOK.

CHRISTIAN THEISM.

A Brief and Popular Survey of the Evidences upon which it rests, and the Objections urged against it considered and refuted. By C. A. Row, M.A. Small 8vo, cloth, $1.75.

"Prebendary Row has attained high repute by his previous publications, but we doubt if he has written anything more likely to be useful than the present volume, in which he sets forth in a popular form and with clearness and force of style the chief reasons on which Christian theistic belief is founded. It is avowedly a popular argument, adapted to the needs of the multitude of people who justly complain that many excellent treatises dealing with the subject are 'over their heads.' It also claims to be a comprehensive survey of the whole question as it is now debated, and grapples with current difficulties and objections which, if they do not subvert the faith of many, do nevertheless prevail with some, and cause widespread disquiet and perplexity."
— *The Standard of the Cross.*

"Among all the works of Prebendary Row in the general line of Apologetics of Christian belief, and they are many, this will be the most prominent in the list, the most thoroughly and lastingly useful."
— *The Living Church.*

BY THE SAME AUTHOR.

REASONS FOR BELIEVING IN CHRISTIANITY. Addressed to busy people. 12mo, cloth, gilt top, 75 cents.

CHRISTIAN EVIDENCE VIEWED IN RELATION TO MODERN THOUGHT. Bampton Lectures for 1877. Fourth Edition. 8vo, cloth, $3.75.

A MANUAL OF CHRISTIAN EVIDENCES. 16mo, cloth, 75 cents.

FUTURE RETRIBUTION, VIEWED IN THE LIGHT OF REASON AND REVELATION. 8vo, cloth, $2.50.

THOMAS WHITTAKER,
2 AND 3 BIBLE HOUSE, NEW YORK.

ON ROMANISM.

Three articles on Romanism. By the Rev. JOHN HENRY HOPKINS, S.T.D. With a useful Index. 12mo, cloth, $1.00.

"Entertaining reading, without a dull line."—*The Churchman.*

"This is a caustic, severe and able arraignment of Romanism."
—*Zion's Herald.*

"Dr. Hopkins' articles form a strong and well stated summary of the question."—*The Critic.*

"An amazingly brilliant book is this. As far as the correspondence with and strictures on Monsignor Capel go, we do not wonder that Dr. Hopkins has republished the whole and wound it up with a snapper in the shape of his elaborate review of Dr. Littledale triumphant, on the 'Petrine Claims.' To outside readers who are not too much enmeshed in Roman Catholic sympathies to be able to extract any kind of enjoyment from the routing of such a serene example of prelatic assumption as Monsignor Capel, the whole will be as good as a play."—*Independent.*

"The discussion is exceedingly sharp and lays bare the tremendous assumptions of the papacy in regard to the authority of the Pope, and the sole right of the Roman Church to the name *Catholic.*"
—*The Lutheran.*

"Dr. Hopkins is bold and sharp, fears nothing, and is especially pointed in detecting weak places in an adversary."—*Public Opinion.*

THOMAS WHITTAKER,

2 AND 3 BIBLE HOUSE, NEW YORK.

www.ingramcontent.com/pod-product-compliance
Lightning Source LLC
Chambersburg PA
CBHW031439160426
43195CB00010BB/786